Materia Medica of Homeopathic Gemstones: Volume Four

Dr Víctor Denis Purcell and Victor Denis Purcell

Published by Dr Víctor Denis Purcell, 2024.

MATERIA MEDICA OF HOMEOPATHIC GEMSTONES: VOLUME FOUR

First edition. July 30, 2024.

Copyright © 2024 Dr Víctor Denis Purcell and Victor Denis Purcell.

ISBN: 979-8227851369

Written by Dr Víctor Denis Purcell and Victor Denis Purcell.

Dedication: Tayler, Matt and Marco and Alexander

Volume Four

Materia Medica of Homeopathic Gemstones

Chapter Listing:

- Chapter 1:introduction to homeopathic medicine

- Chapter 2: Materia Medica

Disclaimer ◈

Please read the following terms and conditions carefully before proceeding.

General Information Purposes Only: The information provided in the following is for general information and entertainment purposes only. All information is provided in good faith; however, the author makes no representation or warranty of any kind, express or implied, regarding the accuracy, adequacy, validity, reliability, availability, or completeness of any information on the following.

Not Medical Advice: The content provided below is not intended to be a substitute for professional medical advice, diagnosis, or treatment. Always seek the advice of your physician or other qualified health providers with any questions you may have regarding a medical condition or health concerns.

No Doctor-Patient Relationship: reading the information below does not constitute establishing a doctor-patient relationship. Any health information communicated is not an endorsement, diagnosis, or treatment regimen.

Professional Assistance: You must not rely on the information below as an alternative to medical advice from your doctor or other professional healthcare providers. If you believe you are experiencing any medical condition, seek immediate medical attention from a licensed healthcare provider.

Risks of Self-Diagnosis: Self-diagnosis can lead to harm, and healthcare professionals must perform diagnosis and treatment.

Limitation of Warranties: The medical information provided is "as is" without any representations or warranties, express or implied. The author makes no representations or warranties concerning the medical report.

Liability: You agree to release the author from all liability and to hold him harmless from any legal claims related to the medical information provided.

Contact a doctor: Do not disregard, avoid, or delay obtaining medical advice from a qualified healthcare provider because of something you may have read in this book or below.

You do understand and agree to the terms of this disclaimer. If you do not agree with these terms, you are not authorized to obtain information from or otherwise proceed.

- **Chapter 1, introduction to homeopathic medicine**

In the realm of medical sciences, where evidence-based practices and biochemical interventions dominate the landscape, there exists a field that takes a markedly different approach: homeopathic medicine. This discipline, rooted in the late 18th century, was pioneered by Samuel Hahnemann, a German physician disillusioned by the prevailing medical practices of his time. Homeopathy is founded on principles that challenge conventional medical paradigms, particularly the notions of dosage, symptom treatment, and the nature of healing itself.

This chapter seeks to provide an in-depth introduction to the foundational principles, history, and philosophy that constitute the backbone of homeopathic medicine. By delving into the core concepts of "similia similibus curentur" (like cures like) and the use of highly diluted remedies, it aims to shed light on how homeopathy stimulates the body's intrinsic healing responses. The journey begins with an exploration of the rich historical roots of homeopathy, from its inception by Hahnemann to the evolution and adaptation of his principles over time. Understanding this historical context is crucial, as it reveals the motivations and insights that drove Hahnemann to develop a system of medicine that emphasized gentle, individualized care over the often harsh and invasive treatments of his era.

Central to this discussion is the Law of Similars, which posits that substances capable of producing symptoms in healthy individuals can be used to treat similar symptoms in the sick. This principle was a radical departure from the conventional medical practices of Hahnemann's time and continues to be a cornerstone of homeopathic practice. Through meticulous experimentation and documentation, Hahnemann developed a comprehensive materia medica that guides homeopaths in matching patient symptoms with appropriate remedies.

Another key aspect of homeopathy covered in this chapter is the process of potentization and succussion, methods developed by Hahnemann to prepare remedies in a way that enhances their healing properties while minimizing toxicity. This process of serial dilution and vigorous shaking, which imprints the "memory" of the original substance onto the diluent, challenges conventional pharmacological beliefs but remains a fundamental practice in homeopathic medicine.

The chapter also delves into the principle of the minimum dose, which emphasizes using the smallest possible amount of a substance to stimulate a healing response. This approach aims to avoid side effects and supports the body's natural healing processes without overwhelming them. It reflects a broader philosophical stance within homeopathy that respects the body's inherent wisdom and capacity for self-healing.

Furthermore, this chapter highlights the individualized approach of homeopathic treatment. Unlike the standardized protocols of conventional medicine, homeopathy tailors its remedies to the unique physical, emotional, and mental symptoms of each patient. This personalized care extends to chronic and complex conditions, emphasizing a holistic view of health that integrates mental, emotional, and physical well-being.

The concept of vital force, or vital energy, is also examined. This vitalist perspective views health as a state of dynamic equilibrium maintained by an intrinsic energy force, which, when imbalanced, leads to disease. Homeopathic remedies aim to restore balance to this vital force, a concept that aligns with various traditional healing systems around the world.

Lastly, the chapter addresses the Doctrine of Drug Proving, a method by which homeopaths determine the effects of remedies through systematic testing on healthy individuals. This empirical approach ensures that the therapeutic application of remedies is grounded in direct human experience, emphasizing the importance of subjective reports as valuable diagnostic tools.

This chapter provides a comprehensive overview of homeopathy's unique approach to medicine, one that emphasizes gentle, individualized care, the use of minimal doses, and a holistic view of health. By understanding these principles and their historical development, readers will gain insight into the distinct nature of homeopathic practice and its enduring relevance in the broader field of healthcare.

- **Main content:**

As we have seen in the above, in this chapter, we delve into the fundamental principles, history, and philosophy underpinning homeopathic medicine. We explore the core concepts of "similia similibus curentur" (like cures like) and the utilization of highly diluted remedies to stimulate the body's intrinsic healing mechanisms. Additionally, we trace the historical origins of homeopathy, from its inception by Samuel Hahnemann to the evolution and development of his principles. This foundational understanding will provide readers with a comprehensive overview of this distinct form of medicine.

The Genesis of Homeopathy: Samuel Hahnemann's Vision

The genesis of homeopathy is rooted in the work of Samuel Hahnemann, an 18th-century German physician. Disenchanted with the medical practices of his time—often characterized by harsh and ineffective treatments—Hahnemann sought a more humane and rational approach to healing. His pursuit led to the principle of "similia similibus curentur" or "like cures like," which became the cornerstone of homeopathic medicine. This principle marked a significant departure from the prevailing medical practices of bloodletting, purging, and the use of toxic substances. Hahnemann envisioned a medical system that supported the body's natural healing tendencies, a concept he found echoed in ancient texts but not rigorously applied in a systematic medical framework.

Hahnemann's early life and education were instrumental in shaping his medical philosophy. Born in 1755 in Meissen, Germany, he exhibited a keen intellect and a passion for learning. He studied medicine at the University of Leipzig and later at the University of Erlangen, where he was awarded his MD. His dissatisfaction with the crude and often harmful medical practices of his time drove him to seek alternatives. His profound knowledge of chemistry, pharmacology, and various languages allowed him to access a broad range of medical texts, further fueling his quest for a better healing system.

The Law of Similars: Understanding "Like Cures Like"

The foundational principle of homeopathy, "like cures like," posits that substances capable of causing disease symptoms in healthy individuals can treat similar symptoms in the sick. Hahnemann's discovery was catalyzed by his observation of the effects of cinchona bark (quinine) in treating malaria, noting that it produced malaria-like symptoms in healthy individuals. This observation led to further experimentation and the formulation of a doctrine suggesting that substances inducing symptoms in healthy individuals could be used to stimulate the body's healing processes. This law signified a profound interconnectedness between humans and nature, which homeopathy seeks to harness.

As Hahnemann continued his experiments, he documented the specific effects of various substances on healthy individuals, a process termed "provings." Volunteers, including Hahnemann himself, would ingest a substance and meticulously record the resulting physical, emotional, and mental symptoms. These observations formed the rudimentary materia medica of homeopathy, guiding the selection of remedies to match a patient's symptom profile.

Hahnemann further refined the preparation of homeopathic remedies through a method known as potentization, which involves systematic dilution and succussion (vigorous shaking) at each dilution step. He proposed that this process not only reduced the toxicity of the substance but also enhanced its therapeutic properties, even when diluted beyond the point of containing any molecules of the original substance. Hahnemann's work with provings extended over many years and involved a wide range of substances, including plants, minerals, and animal products. His dedication to rigorously testing these substances on himself and other volunteers provided a wealth of empirical data that formed the backbone of homeopathic practice.

Individualized treatment is another pivotal element of homeopathy. Unlike the one-size-fits-all approach of conventional medicine, homeopathy emphasizes the uniqueness of each patient's illness experience. Effective treatment requires a thorough understanding of the patient's symptoms, lifestyle, and psychological state, acknowledging the complexity of human health and tailoring remedies to the individual rather than the disease.

This holistic approach extends to the mental and emotional aspects of health. Hahnemann observed that emotional states such as grief or shock could significantly impact physical health, a perspective that was innovative for his time. Homeopathy views disease as a disturbance of the body's vital force, with remedies aiming to stimulate this vital energy to restore balance and health.

The practice of homeopathy spread as Hahnemann's students and followers continued to practice and teach his methods. By the early 19th century, homeopathy had taken root in Europe and America, offering a gentler alternative to the often harsh and invasive medical practices of the time. Hahnemann's meticulous documentation and the publication of his works, such as "The Organon of the Healing Art," played a crucial role in disseminating his ideas. The "Organon" outlined the principles of homeopathy and provided practical guidelines for its practice, becoming the foundational text for homeopathic practitioners.

The Art of Dilution: Potentization and Succussion

In homeopathy, potentization and succession are pivotal processes transforming substances into therapeutic agents. Potentization involves systematic dilution, often to a point where no molecules of the starting material are detectable, combined with succession to transfer the substance's essence or 'energy' into the medium (water or alcohol). Hahnemann developed these methods to mitigate the toxic effects observed with undiluted substances, discovering that the curative properties persisted and were even enhanced through dilution and succussion.

This methodology challenges conventional pharmacology, which relies on dose-dependent effects. The theory behind potentization suggests that the process imprints the memory of the substance onto the diluent, interacting with the body's vital force. Each level of dilution, known as potency, is marked by a specific ratio, and the choice of potency is tailored to the individual patient based on their symptoms.

Succussion is believed to activate the medicinal properties of the solution. Despite skepticism from mainstream science regarding the mechanisms by which succussion enhances therapeutic efficacy, practitioners and patients attest to its qualitative difference, suggesting that shaking is integral to remedy preparation.

The concept of potentization extends beyond remedy preparation to reflect a broader holistic approach. It underscores that the remedy's effectiveness lies not only in its substance but also in its preparation and administration, emphasizing a process-oriented approach to healing. Hahnemann's theory of potentization was not static; he continued to refine and improve his methods throughout his life. His later works, such as the sixth edition of "The Organon," introduced the concept of using even higher dilutions (LM potencies), which he believed could achieve deeper and more lasting healing effects.

Potentization also embodies the homeopathic respect for the complexity and sensitivity of the body. It operates on the understanding that very subtle triggers can activate the body's healing mechanisms and that these mechanisms are capable of profound responses. The tailored potencies speak to this sensitivity, offering a spectrum of stimuli that can be matched to the individual's health and vitality.

The Principle of the Minimum Dose

The principle of the minimum dose in homeopathy posits that the lowest amount of a substance needed to initiate a healing response is the most desirable dosage. This principle aims to avoid side effects and supports the body's natural healing processes without overpowering or suppressing them. Hahnemann sought a gentle and respectful approach to healing, contrasting with the harsh methods of conventional treatments.

The minimum dose principle operates in tandem with potentization to produce remedies interacting with the body's vital force rather than directly affecting its physiology. The goal is to provide enough stimulus for the body's healing response without causing aggravation, reflecting a patient-centered approach that respects the body's pace and capacity for recovery.

Critics argue that minute doses, often beyond the presence of the original substance, cannot have any effect. However, homeopaths assert that clinical outcomes justify their approach, calling for an expanded understanding of drug action beyond material dose-response relationships.

The principle of the minimum dose also speaks to a philosophical stance recognizing the body as a self-healing organism, with medicine supporting rather than usurping the healing process. This principle remains a cornerstone of homeopathic medicine, emphasizing gentle intervention and respect for the body's inherent healing capabilities. The principle aligns with modern trends towards personalized medicine and the minimization of pharmacological interventions, reflecting a growing recognition of the need for more individualized and less invasive therapeutic approaches.

The Individualized Approach: The Patient as the Central Focus

The individualized approach in homeopathy views each patient as a unique entity requiring a tailored treatment strategy. Unlike the standardized protocols of conventional medicine, homeopathy emphasizes comprehensive assessment of the patient's physical, emotional, and mental symptoms, along with their medical history and life circumstances.

This approach demands thorough case-taking, with homeopaths conducting in-depth interviews to understand the patient's subtle symptoms and responses to various influences. The detailed questioning explores aspects such as food preferences, sleep patterns, and emotional temperament, which are crucial in selecting the most fitting remedy.

The individualized approach acknowledges the complexity of the human condition, respecting that the manifestations of illness are as diverse as the people experiencing them. Effective treatment must resonate with the patient's overall well-being, stimulating the body's healing processes in alignment with the individual's vitality and health.

Homeopaths view this approach to honor the whole person, addressing mental and emotional health as integral components of overall well-being. This dynamic process is responsive to changes in the patient's symptoms and health status, allowing for a flexible and evolving treatment strategy. This individualization extends to chronic conditions, where homeopaths may adjust remedies over time to reflect the shifting nature of the patient's health and circumstances.

Moreover, the individualized approach in homeopathy involves creating a therapeutic partnership between the practitioner and the patient. Homeopaths invest significant time in understanding the patient's life story, experiences, and personality traits, fostering a deeper connection that enhances the healing process. This relationship is built on trust, empathy, and mutual respect, providing a supportive environment for patients to engage actively in their healing journey.

The Holistic Philosophy: Treating the Whole Person

The holistic philosophy in homeopathy involves treating the individual in their entirety, considering the complex interplay between mind, body, and spirit. This approach views symptoms as expressions of the body's attempt to heal itself and emphasizes restoring balance within the whole person.

In practice, this philosophy involves meticulous consideration of the patient's physical symptoms, emotional state, mental health, and life circumstances. Homeopaths believe that emotional disturbances or life stressors can manifest as physical ailments, and vice versa, necessitating a comprehensive evaluation.

By addressing the person, homeopathy aims to bring about a state of harmony where health can flourish on all levels. Remedies are intended to support the body's self-healing mechanisms, encouraging a return to balance rather than merely suppressing symptoms.

The holistic approach extends to understanding and treating chronic illnesses, where symptoms can be complex and multifaceted. Homeopathy seeks to understand the underlying patterns of sustaining illness, working towards a sustainable and long-term restoration of health. This approach also involves preventative measures, promoting lifestyle changes that support overall well-being and reduce the likelihood of disease recurrence.

Homeopathy's holistic philosophy aligns with contemporary integrative medicine practices, which advocate for a comprehensive approach to health that includes diet, exercise, stress management, and mental health support. Homeopaths often provide guidance on these aspects, recognizing that a balanced lifestyle is crucial for maintaining health and preventing disease.

The Dynamis Concept: Vital Force as the Essence of Life

The concept of vital force, also known as vital energy, is fundamental to homeopathy's understanding of health and disease. It posits that a dynamic energy force animates all living beings, governing their physical functions and adaptive processes. When this vital force is imbalanced, it leads to symptoms of illness, and homeopathic remedies aim to stimulate this energy to restore balance.

This vitalist perspective differentiates homeopathy from conventional Western medicine, which is primarily mechanical and biochemical. Homeopaths assert that the vital force, although not directly observable, is discernible by its effects. The state of the vital force is reflected in the individual's overall well-being, including their mental, emotional, and physical conditions.

In practice, homeopaths seek to match the remedy's energy with the patient's disturbed vital force. This interaction is believed to stimulate the self-healing process. Symptoms are seen as expressions of a disturbed vital force, guiding the selection of an appropriate remedy to address the underlying imbalance.

The vital force concept is central to homeopathy's holistic treatment of patients, recognizing that symptoms indicate a more profound disturbance rather than merely organ dysfunction. It aligns with other traditional healing systems, such as qi in Traditional Chinese Medicine or prana in Ayurveda, emphasizing the balance of life energy for good health.

Various factors, including emotional states, environmental conditions, and lifestyle choices, influence the strength and harmony of the vital force. Therefore, a homeopath may guide diet, stress management, and other aspects of life that can support the patient's vitality. Maintaining a robust and balanced vital force is critical to resilience against illness.

In dealing with chronic diseases, the concept of the vital force is particularly significant. Homeopaths consider the long-term vitality and energy patterns of the individual, aiming to gradually restore the disturbed vital force to a state of equilibrium. Chronic symptoms indicate a deep-seated imbalance in the vital force that requires a sustained therapeutic strategy.

The vital force concept also informs the homeopathic perspective on prevention. A well-balanced vital energy confers immunity and resilience, reducing disease susceptibility. Thus, homeopathy places a strong emphasis on strengthening the vital force as a means of preventing illness and promoting long-term health.

The Principle of Potentization: Unlocking Remedial Energy

The principle of potentization is a hallmark of homeopathy, representing a unique process by which remedies are prepared to enhance their healing properties. This involves serial dilution and succussion (vigorous shaking) of a substance, aiming to release its energetic potential. Homeopaths believe this process amplifies the remedy's therapeutic qualities, stimulating the body's vital force while minimizing toxic side effects.

Potentization challenges conventional dose-response relationships, suggesting that the therapeutic qualities of a substance can operate at a level subtler than the molecular or chemical. The process is thought to imprint the substance's "memory" onto the diluent, with each dilution and succussion step increasing this energetic imprint.

The choice of potency is critical and tailored to each patient, considering factors such as sensitivity, illness nature, and symptom duration. The meticulous preparation of remedies reflects homeopathy's respect for both the material and non-material aspects of healing.

Potentization is not merely a means of remedy preparation but also a philosophical stance on the nature of medicine and healing. It posits that energy and information are central to health and that substances have capacities beyond their chemical composition. These principles challenge conventional medical paradigms and invite a broader understanding of what is therapeutically possible.

Homeopaths argue that potentization allows for a more precise and personalized approach to treatment. By selecting the appropriate potency, practitioners can tailor the remedy to the individual needs of the patient, ensuring that the treatment is both effective and gentle.

This personalized approach is a testament to the detailed nature of homeopathic practice and its commitment to individualized care.

The Doctrine of Drug Proving: Understanding Remedies through Human Experience

The Doctrine of Drug Proving is fundamental to homeopathy, whereby substances are systematically tested on healthy individuals to determine the range of symptoms they produce. These symptoms are meticulously cataloged to create detailed remedy profiles, ensuring therapeutic applications are grounded in empirical observation and direct human experience.

Drug proving involves healthy volunteers taking a homeopathic potency of a substance and recording all changes experienced. These self-observations contribute to the homeopathic materia medica, guiding the selection of remedies to match patient symptoms.

The methodology emphasizes safety, with remedies used in highly diluted forms to minimize adverse effects. Drug proving reflects homeopathy's empirical approach, respecting the nuances of human experiences and emphasizing the importance of subjective reports as valuable diagnostic tools.

The records from drug provings are compiled and scrutinized by homeopaths to discern patterns and characteristic symptoms that are consistently produced by the substance. These typical symptoms become essential in the homeopathic prescription process as they guide the practitioner in matching a patient's symptoms with the remedy profile.

The Doctrine of Drug Proving is also a testament to the homeopathic respect for the subtlety of human perception and the complexity of human experiences. Unlike conventional trials that may dismiss subjective experiences as irrelevant or anecdotal, homeopathy values these personal reports as essential data for understanding the multi-dimensional impact of remedies.

Drug proving is an ongoing process, reflecting homeopathy's openness to discovering new remedies and expanding its materia medica. As society encounters new substances and our environments change, homeopathy recognizes the need to explore and understand the healing potential of new agents continuously.

Summary of this chapter

Homeopathic medicine represents a unique and distinct paradigm within the broader field of medical sciences, characterized by its foundational principles, historical context, and philosophical underpinnings. This summary provides a comprehensive overview of the salient features of homeopathy, reflecting its evolution and enduring relevance in contemporary healthcare.

Homeopathy originated in the late 18th century through the pioneering work of Samuel Hahnemann, a German physician who sought alternatives to the harsh and often ineffective medical practices of his time. Dissatisfied with conventional treatments such as bloodletting and purging, Hahnemann formulated the principle of "similia similibus curentur" or "like cures like." This doctrine posits that substances capable of producing symptoms in healthy individuals can be utilized to treat similar symptoms in the sick, thus stimulating the body's intrinsic healing mechanisms. This foundational concept marked a significant departure from the prevailing medical theories and practices, setting the stage for the development of a new therapeutic system.

Central to homeopathy is the process of potentization, which involves the serial dilution and succussion (vigorous shaking) of substances to enhance their therapeutic properties while minimizing toxicity. This method, which imprints the "memory" of the original substance onto the diluent, challenges conventional pharmacological principles. However, it remains a cornerstone of homeopathic practice, reflecting a nuanced understanding of the interplay between substance, energy, and the body's vital force.

The principle of the minimum dose further distinguishes homeopathy from conventional medicine. By advocating for the smallest possible amount of a substance to elicit a healing response, homeopathy emphasizes a gentle, patient-centered approach that avoids overwhelming the body's natural processes. This minimalistic strategy aligns with a broader philosophical stance that respects the body's inherent wisdom and self-regulatory capabilities.

Homeopathy's individualized approach to treatment underscores its commitment to personalized care. Unlike standardized protocols in conventional medicine, homeopathy tailors its remedies to the unique constellation of physical, emotional, and mental symptoms presented by each patient. This holistic perspective integrates various dimensions of health, recognizing the interconnectedness of the mind, body, and spirit. Such an approach is particularly valuable in managing chronic and complex conditions, where a deeper understanding of the patient's overall well-being is paramount.

The concept of vital force, or vital energy, is integral to homeopathy's theoretical framework. This vitalist perspective posits that health is maintained by a dynamic equilibrium of intrinsic energy, which, when disrupted, manifests as disease. Homeopathic remedies aim to restore balance to this vital force, a notion that resonates with various traditional healing systems worldwide, such as qi in Traditional Chinese Medicine and prana in Ayurveda.

The empirical basis of homeopathy is further reinforced by the Doctrine of Drug Proving. This methodology involves systematically testing substances on healthy individuals to document the full spectrum of symptoms they produce. These detailed observations form the materia medica, guiding practitioners in selecting remedies that match the patient's symptom profile. This rigorous, experiential approach underscores the importance of subjective reports as valuable diagnostic tools and ensures that homeopathic treatments are grounded in direct human experience.

In conclusion, homeopathic medicine offers a distinctive and holistic approach to healthcare, emphasizing individualized treatment, minimal dosing, and the restoration of vital force. Its principles challenge conventional medical paradigms, advocating for a patient-centered, gentle, and integrative approach to healing. By understanding these foundational concepts and their historical evolution, one gains a deeper appreciation of homeopathy's role and potential within the broader landscape of medical practice. This comprehensive overview underscores the enduring relevance and adaptability of homeopathic principles in addressing contemporary health challenges, reflecting a commitment to a more personalized and holistic vision of health and well-being.

- **Chapter 2: Materia Medica**

Wavellite: Comprehensive Guide on Spiritual and Physical Healing Properties

Overview

Wavellite, a hydrous phosphate mineral, is recognized for its radial crystal formations and diverse color range, from green to yellow and white. Found primarily in the USA and Brazil, this mineral is valued for its ability to promote clarity and provide emotional healing.

Spiritual and Psychic Benefits

Clarity: Wavellite is celebrated for its ability to clear mental fog and enhance cognitive function. It helps improve focus, concentration, and memory, making it ideal for those seeking mental sharpness.

Emotional Healing: This gemstone provides strong emotional healing, helping individuals to process and release negative emotions. It fosters a sense of calm and stability.

Spiritual Awareness: Wavellite enhances spiritual awareness and enlightenment. It helps individuals connect with their inner wisdom and access higher levels of consciousness.

Intuition and Insight: Wavellite boosts intuition and insight, aiding individuals in understanding the deeper meanings of life and their experiences.

Protection: Known for its protective properties, Wavellite shields individuals from negative influences and emotional stress. It creates a safe and harmonious environment.

Physical Healing Properties

Immune System Support: Wavellite is believed to support the immune system, helping the body to fight off infections and diseases. It promotes overall immune health and vitality.

Pain Relief: This gemstone provides relief from physical pain, particularly in conditions related to inflammation and tension. It helps to reduce discomfort and promote overall physical well-being.

Detoxification: Wavellite aids in the detoxification process, supporting the body's natural ability to eliminate toxins. It enhances liver and kidney function, promoting overall metabolic health and efficient waste removal.

Respiratory Health: Wavellite supports respiratory health, helping to alleviate symptoms of lung-related conditions and improve overall lung function.

Circulatory Health: Wavellite supports circulatory health, improving blood flow and reducing the risk of cardiovascular issues. It helps to maintain a healthy heart and vascular system.

Potential Homeopathic Uses

If Wavellite were to be used as a homeopathic remedy, its indications might include:

Psychological Symptoms: Anxiety, emotional stress, and mental confusion. It may also help in cases of emotional detachment and isolation.

Physical Symptoms: Immune system deficiencies, respiratory issues, and detoxification needs.

Behavioral Symptoms: Difficulty in managing stress, susceptibility to negative influences, and a need for emotional healing.

Wavellite's homeopathic profile would focus on its ability to clarify, protect, and detoxify, making it suitable for addressing conditions related to mental and physical well-being.

Conclusion

Wavellite is a vital crystal in holistic healing, celebrated for its unique properties and healing energies. Whether used for mental clarity, emotional healing, or physical health, Wavellite serves as a potent aid in achieving overall well-being and harmony. As with all alternative practices, these should be considered as complementary to conventional medical treatments.

Xanadu: Comprehensive Guide on Spiritual and Physical Healing Properties

Overview

Xanadu, an exotic and rare gemstone, is recognized for its mesmerizing blue-green hues and extraordinary healing properties. Found primarily in China and the USA, this mineral is highly valued for its ability to promote emotional balance and enhance spiritual connection.

Spiritual and Psychic Benefits

Emotional Balance: Xanadu is celebrated for its ability to stabilize emotions and promote a sense of inner peace. It helps to release negative emotions and fosters a positive outlook on life.

Spiritual Connection: This gemstone enhances spiritual connection and awareness. It helps individuals align with their higher selves and access deeper levels of consciousness.

Protection: Xanadu provides strong protective energies, shielding individuals from negative influences and harmful energies. It is particularly useful for those who seek to create a safe and harmonious environment.

Harmony and Balance: Xanadu promotes harmony and balance in all aspects of life. It helps to align the chakras and stabilize the mood, fostering a sense of well-being and tranquility.

Prosperity and Abundance: Known for attracting prosperity and abundance, Xanadu is often used in rituals and practices to manifest wealth and success. It encourages a positive mindset and helps to remove obstacles to achieving one's goals.

Physical Healing Properties

Kidney Health: Xanadu is known to support kidney health, helping to improve kidney function and detoxify the body. It is beneficial for those dealing with kidney-related issues.

Immune System Support: Xanadu enhances the immune system, helping the body to fight off infections and diseases. It promotes overall immune health and vitality.

Pain Relief: This gemstone provides relief from physical pain, particularly in conditions related to inflammation and tension. It helps to reduce discomfort and promote overall physical well-being.

Heart Health: Xanadu supports heart health, improving circulation and reducing the risk of cardiovascular issues. It helps to maintain a healthy heart and vascular system.

Detoxification: Xanadu aids in the detoxification process, supporting the body's natural ability to eliminate toxins. It enhances liver and kidney function, promoting overall metabolic health and efficient waste removal.

Potential Homeopathic Uses

If Xanadu were to be used as a homeopathic remedy, its indications might include:

Psychological Symptoms: Anxiety, emotional stress, and mood swings. It may also help in cases of emotional detachment and isolation.

Physical Symptoms: Kidney-related issues, immune system deficiencies, and cardiovascular health.

Behavioral Symptoms: Difficulty in managing stress, susceptibility to negative influences, and a need for emotional balance.

Xanadu's homeopathic profile would focus on its ability to balance, protect, and detoxify, making it suitable for addressing conditions related to emotional and physical well-being.

Conclusion

Xanadu is a vital crystal in holistic healing, celebrated not just for its beauty but for its versatile healing properties. Whether used for emotional balance, spiritual connection, or physical health, Xanadu serves as a potent aid in achieving overall well-being and harmony. Like all alternative practices, these should be considered as complementary to conventional medical treatments.

Yttrium: Comprehensive Guide on Spiritual and Physical Healing Properties

Overview

Yttrium, a rare earth element, is recognized for its silvery-white appearance and powerful healing properties. Found primarily in China and the USA, this mineral is highly valued for its ability to enhance mental clarity and provide physical rejuvenation.

Spiritual and Psychic Benefits

Mental Clarity: Yttrium is celebrated for its ability to clear mental fog and enhance cognitive function. It helps improve focus, concentration, and memory, making it ideal for those seeking mental sharpness.

Emotional Stability: This mineral provides strong emotional stability, helping individuals to process and release negative emotions. It fosters a sense of calm and balance.

Spiritual Growth: Yttrium enhances spiritual growth and awareness. It helps individuals connect with their inner wisdom and access higher levels of consciousness.

Protection: Known for its protective properties, Yttrium shields individuals from negative influences and emotional stress. It creates a safe and harmonious environment.

Energy Amplification: Yttrium is known for its ability to amplify energy, enhancing the effects of other healing crystals and personal energy.

Physical Healing Properties

Immune System Support: Yttrium is believed to support the immune system, helping the body to fight off infections and diseases. It promotes overall immune health and vitality.

Pain Relief: This mineral provides relief from physical pain, particularly in conditions related to inflammation and tension. It helps to reduce discomfort and promote overall physical well-being.

Detoxification: Yttrium aids in the detoxification process, supporting the body's natural ability to eliminate toxins. It enhances liver and kidney function, promoting overall metabolic health and efficient waste removal.

Bone Health: Yttrium supports bone health, helping to strengthen bones and prevent fractures. It is beneficial for those dealing with bone-related issues.

Circulatory Health: Yttrium supports circulatory health, improving blood flow and reducing the risk of cardiovascular issues. It helps to maintain a healthy heart and vascular system.

Potential Homeopathic Uses

If Yttrium were to be used as a homeopathic remedy, its indications might include:

Psychological Symptoms: Anxiety, emotional stress, and mental confusion. It may also help in cases of emotional detachment and isolation.

Physical Symptoms: Immune system deficiencies, bone health support, and detoxification needs.

Behavioral Symptoms: Difficulty in managing stress, susceptibility to negative influences, and a need for mental clarity.

Yttrium's homeopathic profile would focus on its ability to clarify, protect, and rejuvenate, making it suitable for addressing conditions related to mental and physical well-being.

Conclusion

Yttrium is a powerful mineral in holistic healing, celebrated for its unique properties and healing energies. Whether used for mental clarity, emotional stability, or physical health, Yttrium serves as a potent aid in achieving overall well-being and harmony. As with all alternative practices, these should be considered as complementary to conventional medical treatments.

Zinkenite: Comprehensive Guide on Spiritual and Physical Healing Properties

Overview

Zinkenite, a rare sulfide mineral, is recognized for its metallic silver-gray color and unique healing properties. Found primarily in Bolivia and Romania, this mineral is valued for its ability to enhance mental focus and provide emotional grounding.

Spiritual and Psychic Benefits

Mental Focus: Zinkenite is celebrated for its ability to improve mental clarity and focus. It helps to enhance concentration and memory, making it ideal for those who need to maintain mental sharpness.

Emotional Grounding: This gemstone provides strong emotional grounding, helping individuals to stay balanced and centered. It is particularly useful for those who feel overwhelmed by their emotions.

Spiritual Awareness: Zinkenite enhances spiritual awareness and helps individuals connect with their inner selves. It aids in deepening one's spiritual practice and understanding.

Protection: Known for its protective properties, Zinkenite shields individuals from negative energies and emotional stress. It creates a safe and harmonious environment.

Stability and Balance: Zinkenite promotes stability and balance in all aspects of life. It helps to align the chakras and stabilize the mood, fostering a sense of well-being and tranquility.

Physical Healing Properties

Immune System Support: Zinkenite is believed to support the immune system, helping the body to fight off infections and diseases. It promotes overall immune health and vitality.

Pain Relief: This gemstone provides relief from physical pain, particularly in conditions related to inflammation and tension. It helps to reduce discomfort and promote overall physical well-being.

Detoxification: Zinkenite aids in the detoxification process, supporting the body's natural ability to eliminate toxins. It enhances liver and kidney function, promoting overall metabolic health and efficient waste removal.

Respiratory Health: Zinkenite supports respiratory health, helping to alleviate symptoms of lung-related conditions and improve overall lung function.

Circulatory Health: Zinkenite supports circulatory health, improving blood flow and reducing the risk of cardiovascular issues. It helps to maintain a healthy heart and vascular system.

Potential Homeopathic Uses

If Zinkenite were to be used as a homeopathic remedy, its indications might include:

Psychological Symptoms: Anxiety, emotional stress, and mental confusion. It may also help in cases of emotional detachment and isolation.

Physical Symptoms: Immune system deficiencies, respiratory issues, and detoxification needs.

Behavioral Symptoms: Difficulty in managing stress, susceptibility to negative influences, and a need for emotional grounding.

Zinkenite's homeopathic profile would focus on its ability to focus, protect, and detoxify, making it suitable for addressing conditions related to mental and physical well-being.

Conclusion

Zinkenite is a powerful crystal in holistic healing, celebrated for its unique properties and grounding energies. Whether used for mental focus, emotional grounding, or physical health, Zinkenite serves as a potent aid in achieving overall well-being and harmony. As with all alternative practices, these should be considered as complementary to conventional medical treatments.

Zincite: Comprehensive Guide on Spiritual and Physical Healing Properties

Overview

Zincite, a rare zinc oxide mineral, is recognized for its vibrant colors, ranging from red to orange and yellow, and its powerful healing properties. Found primarily in Poland and the USA, this mineral is highly valued for its ability to enhance vitality and promote emotional healing.

Spiritual and Psychic Benefits

Vitality and Energy: Zincite is celebrated for its ability to boost energy levels and enhance vitality. It helps to invigorate the body and mind, making it ideal for those who need an energy boost.

Emotional Healing: This gemstone provides strong emotional healing, helping individuals to process and release negative emotions. It fosters a sense of calm and stability.

Spiritual Growth: Zincite enhances spiritual growth and transformation. It helps individuals connect with their higher selves and access deeper levels of consciousness.

Protection: Known for its protective properties, Zincite shields individuals from negative influences and emotional stress. It creates a safe and harmonious environment.

Creativity and Inspiration: Zincite is known for its ability to stimulate creativity and inspiration. It helps to unlock creative potential and encourages innovative thinking.

Physical Healing Properties

Immune System Support: Zincite is believed to support the immune system, helping the body to fight off infections and diseases. It promotes overall immune health and vitality.

Pain Relief: This gemstone provides relief from physical pain, particularly in conditions related to inflammation and tension. It helps to reduce discomfort and promote overall physical well-being.

Detoxification: Zincite aids in the detoxification process, supporting the body's natural ability to eliminate toxins. It enhances

liver and kidney function, promoting overall metabolic health and efficient waste removal.

Respiratory Health: Zincite supports respiratory health, helping to alleviate symptoms of lung-related conditions and improve overall lung function.

Circulatory Health: Zincite supports circulatory health, improving blood flow and reducing the risk of cardiovascular issues. It helps to maintain a healthy heart and vascular system.

Potential Homeopathic Uses

If Zincite were to be used as a homeopathic remedy, its indications might include:

Psychological Symptoms: Anxiety, emotional stress, and mental confusion. It may also help in cases of emotional detachment and isolation.

Physical Symptoms: Immune system deficiencies, respiratory issues, and detoxification needs.

Behavioral Symptoms: Difficulty in managing stress, susceptibility to negative influences, and a need for vitality and energy.

Zincite's homeopathic profile would focus on its ability to energize, protect, and detoxify, making it suitable for addressing conditions related to mental and physical well-being.

Conclusion

Zincite is a vital crystal in holistic healing, celebrated for its unique properties and healing energies. Whether used for vitality, emotional healing, or physical health, Zincite serves as a potent aid in achieving overall well-being and harmony. As with all alternative practices, these should be considered as complementary to conventional medical treatments.

Zirconolite: Comprehensive Guide on Spiritual and Physical Healing Properties

Overview

Zirconolite, a rare complex oxide mineral, is recognized for its black to brownish-black color and unique healing properties. Found primarily in Norway and the USA, this mineral is valued for its ability to enhance grounding and provide protective energies.

Spiritual and Psychic Benefits

Grounding: Zirconolite is celebrated for its ability to ground individuals, helping them stay connected to the earth. It is particularly useful for those who feel scattered or disconnected from their physical environment.

Protection: This gemstone provides strong protective energies, shielding individuals from negative influences and emotional stress. It creates a safe and harmonious environment.

Emotional Stability: Zirconolite promotes emotional stability and resilience. It helps to balance mood swings and provides a sense of calm and composure, making it easier to manage stress and emotional turmoil.

Spiritual Awareness: Zirconolite enhances spiritual awareness and helps individuals connect with their inner selves. It aids in deepening one's spiritual practice and understanding.

Energy Regulation: Known for its complex structure, Zirconolite helps to regulate and balance personal energy. It enhances the body's natural energy flow, promoting overall well-being.

Physical Healing Properties

Immune System Support: Zirconolite is believed to support the immune system, helping the body to fight off infections and diseases. It promotes overall immune health and vitality.

Pain Relief: This gemstone provides relief from physical pain, particularly in conditions related to inflammation and tension. It helps to reduce discomfort and promote overall physical well-being.

Detoxification: Zirconolite aids in the detoxification process, supporting the body's natural ability to eliminate toxins. It enhances

liver and kidney function, promoting overall metabolic health and efficient waste removal.

Respiratory Health: Zirconolite supports respiratory health, helping to alleviate symptoms of lung-related conditions and improve overall lung function.

Circulatory Health: Zirconolite supports circulatory health, improving blood flow and reducing the risk of cardiovascular issues. It helps to maintain a healthy heart and vascular system.

Potential Homeopathic Uses

If Zirconolite were to be used as a homeopathic remedy, its indications might include:

Psychological Symptoms: Anxiety, emotional stress, and mental confusion. It may also help in cases of emotional detachment and isolation.

Physical Symptoms: Immune system deficiencies, respiratory issues, and detoxification needs.

Behavioral Symptoms: Difficulty in managing stress, susceptibility to negative influences, and a need for grounding.

Zirconolite's homeopathic profile would focus on its ability to ground, protect, and detoxify, making it suitable for addressing conditions related to mental and physical well-being.

Conclusion

Zirconolite is a powerful crystal in holistic healing, celebrated for its unique properties and grounding energies. Whether used for grounding, emotional stability, or physical health, Zirconolite serves as a potent aid in achieving overall well-being and harmony. As with all alternative practices, these should be considered as complementary to conventional medical treatments.

Zoisite: Comprehensive Guide on Spiritual and Physical Healing Properties

Overview

Zoisite, a member of the epidote group, is recognized for its vibrant colors, ranging from green to pink and blue. Found primarily in Tanzania and India, this mineral is highly valued for its ability to promote emotional healing and enhance spiritual growth.

Spiritual and Psychic Benefits

Emotional Healing: Zoisite is celebrated for its profound ability to heal emotional wounds and trauma. It helps release past emotional pain and fosters forgiveness and compassion.

Spiritual Growth: This gemstone enhances spiritual growth and transformation. It helps individuals connect with their higher selves and access deeper levels of consciousness.

Intuition and Insight: Zoisite enhances intuition and insight, helping individuals see beyond the surface of situations and people. It aids in discerning the truth and provides clarity in complex situations.

Calm and Tranquility: Zoisite promotes a sense of calm and tranquility. It helps to alleviate feelings of anxiety, stress, and fear, providing a sense of peace and security.

Courage and Confidence: Known for its ability to boost confidence and courage, Zoisite empowers individuals to take bold steps towards their goals. It encourages a positive outlook and helps build self-assurance.

Physical Healing Properties

Immune System Support: Zoisite is known to support the immune system, helping the body to fight off infections and diseases. It promotes overall immune health and enhances the body's natural defenses.

Pain Relief: Zoisite provides relief from physical pain, particularly in conditions related to inflammation and tension. It helps to reduce discomfort and promote overall physical well-being.

Detoxification: This gemstone aids in the detoxification process, supporting the body's natural ability to eliminate toxins. It enhances

liver and kidney function, promoting overall metabolic health and efficient waste removal.

Respiratory Health: Zoisite supports respiratory health, helping to alleviate symptoms of lung-related conditions and improve overall lung function.

Circulatory Health: Zoisite supports circulatory health, improving blood flow and reducing the risk of cardiovascular issues. It helps to maintain a healthy heart and vascular system.

Potential Homeopathic Uses

If Zoisite were to be used as a homeopathic remedy, its indications might include:

Psychological Symptoms: Anxiety, emotional stress, and trauma. It may also help in cases of emotional detachment and isolation.

Physical Symptoms: Immune system deficiencies, respiratory issues, and detoxification needs.

Behavioral Symptoms: Difficulty in managing stress, susceptibility to negative influences, and a need for courage and confidence.

Zoisite's homeopathic profile would focus on its ability to heal, protect, and detoxify, making it suitable for addressing conditions related to emotional and physical well-being.

Conclusion

Zoisite is a vital crystal in holistic healing, celebrated for its unique properties and healing energies. Whether used for emotional healing, spiritual growth, or physical health, Zoisite serves as a potent aid in achieving overall well-being and harmony. As with all alternative practices, these should be considered as complementary to conventional medical treatments.

Bastite: Comprehensive Guide on Spiritual and Physical Healing Properties

Overview

Bastite, a variety of serpentine, is recognized for its green hues and unique healing properties. Found primarily in the USA and Canada, this mineral is valued for its ability to enhance emotional stability and promote physical healing.

Spiritual and Psychic Benefits

Emotional Stability: Bastite is celebrated for its ability to stabilize emotions and promote a sense of inner peace. It helps to release negative emotions and fosters a positive outlook on life.

Spiritual Connection: This gemstone enhances spiritual connection and awareness. It helps individuals align with their higher selves and access deeper levels of consciousness.

Protection: Bastite provides strong protective energies, shielding individuals from negative influences and harmful energies. It is particularly useful for those who seek to create a safe and harmonious environment.

Harmony and Balance: Bastite promotes harmony and balance in all aspects of life. It helps to align the chakras and stabilize the mood, fostering a sense of well-being and tranquility.

Grounding: Known for its grounding properties, Bastite helps individuals stay connected to the earth and maintain balance in their lives.

Physical Healing Properties

Immune System Support: Bastite is believed to support the immune system, helping the body to fight off infections and diseases. It promotes overall immune health and vitality.

Pain Relief: This gemstone provides relief from physical pain, particularly in conditions related to inflammation and tension. It helps to reduce discomfort and promote overall physical well-being.

Detoxification: Bastite aids in the detoxification process, supporting the body's natural ability to eliminate toxins. It enhances liver and kidney function, promoting overall metabolic health and efficient waste removal.

Respiratory Health: Bastite supports respiratory health, helping to alleviate symptoms of lung-related conditions and improve overall lung function.

Circulatory Health: Bastite supports circulatory health, improving blood flow and reducing the risk of cardiovascular issues. It helps to maintain a healthy heart and vascular system.

Potential Homeopathic Uses

If Bastite were to be used as a homeopathic remedy, its indications might include:

Psychological Symptoms: Anxiety, emotional stress, and mood swings. It may also help in cases of emotional detachment and isolation.

Physical Symptoms: Immune system deficiencies, respiratory issues, and detoxification needs.

Behavioral Symptoms: Difficulty in managing stress, susceptibility to negative influences, and a need for emotional stability.

Bastite's homeopathic profile would focus on its ability to stabilize, protect, and detoxify, making it suitable for addressing conditions related to emotional and physical well-being.

Conclusion

Bastite is a vital crystal in holistic healing, celebrated for its unique properties and healing energies. Whether used for emotional stability, spiritual connection, or physical health, Bastite serves as a potent aid in achieving overall well-being and harmony. As with all alternative practices, these should be considered as complementary to conventional medical treatments.

Bauxite: Comprehensive Guide on Spiritual and Physical Healing Properties

Overview

Bauxite, the primary ore of aluminum, is recognized for its reddish-brown color and unique healing properties. Found primarily in Australia and Brazil, this mineral is valued for its ability to enhance energy and promote physical healing.

Spiritual and Psychic Benefits

Energy and Vitality: Bauxite is celebrated for its ability to boost energy levels and enhance vitality. It helps to invigorate the body and mind, making it ideal for those who need an energy boost.

Emotional Balance: This gemstone provides strong emotional balance, helping individuals to process and release negative emotions. It fosters a sense of calm and stability.

Spiritual Growth: Bauxite enhances spiritual growth and transformation. It helps individuals connect with their higher selves and access deeper levels of consciousness.

Protection: Known for its protective properties, Bauxite shields individuals from negative influences and emotional stress. It creates a safe and harmonious environment.

Grounding: Bauxite is known for its grounding properties, helping individuals stay connected to the earth and maintain balance in their lives.

Physical Healing Properties

Immune System Support: Bauxite is believed to support the immune system, helping the body to fight off infections and diseases. It promotes overall immune health and vitality.

Pain Relief: This gemstone provides relief from physical pain, particularly in conditions related to inflammation and tension. It helps to reduce discomfort and promote overall physical well-being.

Detoxification: Bauxite aids in the detoxification process, supporting the body's natural ability to eliminate toxins. It enhances liver and kidney function, promoting overall metabolic health and efficient waste removal.

Respiratory Health: Bauxite supports respiratory health, helping to alleviate symptoms of lung-related conditions and improve overall lung function.

Circulatory Health: Bauxite supports circulatory health, improving blood flow and reducing the risk of cardiovascular issues. It helps to maintain a healthy heart and vascular system.

Potential Homeopathic Uses

If Bauxite were to be used as a homeopathic remedy, its indications might include:

Psychological Symptoms: Anxiety, emotional stress, and mental confusion. It may also help in cases of emotional detachment and isolation.

Physical Symptoms: Immune system deficiencies, respiratory issues, and detoxification needs.

Behavioral Symptoms: Difficulty in managing stress, susceptibility to negative influences, and a need for energy and vitality.

Bauxite's homeopathic profile would focus on its ability to energize, protect, and detoxify, making it suitable for addressing conditions related to mental and physical well-being.

Conclusion

Bauxite is a vital crystal in holistic healing, celebrated for its unique properties and healing energies. Whether used for energy, emotional balance, or physical health, Bauxite serves as a potent aid in achieving overall well-being and harmony. As with all alternative practices, these should be considered as complementary to conventional medical treatments.

Chrysoberyl: Comprehensive Guide on Spiritual and Physical Healing Properties

Overview

Chrysoberyl, often recognized for its enchanting yellow-green to golden hues, is a gemstone admired for its unique optical properties and strong energetic vibrations. This crystal is highly valued in various cultures for its ability to enhance personal power, clarity, and protection.

Spiritual and Psychic Benefits

Clarity and Focus: Chrysoberyl is renowned for its ability to clear the mind and sharpen focus. It aids in decision-making and provides mental clarity, making it an excellent stone for students, professionals, and anyone seeking to improve their cognitive abilities.

Spiritual Growth: This gemstone is connected to the solar plexus and heart chakras, promoting personal growth and spiritual evolution. It encourages self-discipline, willpower, and inner strength, facilitating a deeper connection to one's higher self and spiritual path.

Protection: Chrysoberyl is believed to serve as a powerful protective stone, shielding the wearer from negative energies and psychic attacks. It creates a barrier against harmful influences, ensuring a safe and secure energetic environment.

Enhancement of Healing Energies: Known for amplifying healing energies, Chrysoberyl enhances both personal energy and the effectiveness of other healing crystals. It is particularly beneficial in energy healing practices for its ability to stimulate and balance the body's energy centers.

Harmonization and Balance: Chrysoberyl assists in balancing the body's subtle energies. It aligns the chakras and stabilizes emotions, promoting overall well-being and a harmonious internal state.

Versatile Use in Healing Practices: Utilized in various forms such as raw crystals, polished stones, and jewelry, Chrysoberyl is a key component in holistic healing practices. It is often used in meditation and energy healing sessions to enhance spiritual growth and emotional balance.

Physical Healing Properties

Eye Health: Chrysoberyl is believed to support eye health and improve vision. It is said to help with eye-related conditions and enhance visual acuity.

Detoxification: This crystal aids in detoxification by supporting liver function and helping to cleanse the body of toxins. It promotes overall metabolic health and vitality.

Immune System: Chrysoberyl is thought to boost the immune system, helping the body to fight off infections and illnesses more effectively. It supports the body's natural defenses and promotes overall health and vitality.

Energy Balance: By harmonizing the flow of internal energies, Chrysoberyl supports physical and emotional health. It helps in the recovery process from various conditions and promotes overall well-being.

Potential Homeopathic Uses

If Chrysoberyl were to be used as a homeopathic remedy, its indications might include:

Psychological Symptoms: Mental fatigue, lack of focus, and difficulty in making decisions. It may also help in cases of emotional instability and stress.

Physical Symptoms: Eye-related conditions, immune system deficiencies, and metabolic detoxification needs.

Behavioral Symptoms: Procrastination, lack of motivation, and difficulty in managing stress. It may also help with feelings of overwhelm and emotional disturbances.

Chrysoberyl's homeopathic profile would focus on its ability to cleanse, protect, and stabilize, making it suitable for addressing conditions related to mental clarity, energy alignment, and overall health.

Conclusion

Chrysoberyl is a vital gemstone in holistic healing, celebrated not just for its beauty but for its versatile healing properties. Whether used for mental clarity, energy balancing, or as a protective talisman, Chrysoberyl serves as a potent aid in achieving physical health and spiritual harmony. As with all alternative practices, these should be considered complementary to conventional medical treatments.

Danburite: Comprehensive Guide on Spiritual and Physical Healing Properties

Overview

Danburite, a beautiful and radiant gemstone, is treasured for its high vibrational energy and powerful healing properties. Known for its clear to light golden hues, Danburite is a favorite among crystal enthusiasts for its ability to promote emotional healing, spiritual growth, and overall well-being.

Spiritual and Psychic Benefits

Emotional Healing and Calming: Danburite is highly regarded for its ability to soothe emotional pain and reduce stress. It helps to calm the mind and heart, providing relief from anxiety, sadness, and emotional turmoil.

Spiritual Growth: Associated with the crown and heart chakras, Danburite enhances spiritual awareness and enlightenment. It facilitates a stronger connection to higher realms, promoting inner peace and spiritual growth.

Protection: Danburite is believed to offer protection against negative energies and psychic attacks. It creates a shield of light around the wearer, ensuring a safe and positive energetic environment.

Enhancement of Healing Energies: Known for its high vibrational energy, Danburite amplifies personal energy and enhances the effectiveness of other healing crystals. It is particularly beneficial in energy healing practices for its ability to elevate and harmonize the body's energy fields.

Harmonization and Balance: Danburite assists in balancing the body's subtle energies. It aligns the chakras and stabilizes emotions, fostering a harmonious internal state and promoting overall well-being.

Versatile Use in Healing Practices: Utilized in various forms such as raw crystals, polished stones, and jewelry, Danburite is a key component in holistic healing practices. It is often used in meditation and energy healing sessions to enhance spiritual growth and emotional balance.

Physical Healing Properties

Heart Health: Danburite is believed to support heart health and improve cardiovascular function. It is said to help with heart-related conditions and promote overall heart wellness.

Detoxification: This crystal aids in detoxification by supporting the body's natural cleansing processes. It helps to eliminate toxins, promoting overall metabolic health and vitality.

Immune System: Danburite is thought to boost the immune system, helping the body to fight off infections and illnesses more effectively. It supports the body's natural defenses and promotes overall health and vitality.

Energy Balance: By harmonizing the flow of internal energies, Danburite supports physical and emotional health. It helps in the recovery process from various conditions and promotes overall well-being.

Potential Homeopathic Uses

If Danburite were to be used as a homeopathic remedy, its indications might include:

Psychological Symptoms: Anxiety, emotional stress, and feelings of sadness. It may also help in cases of emotional instability and trauma.

Physical Symptoms: Heart-related conditions, immune system deficiencies, and metabolic detoxification needs.

Behavioral Symptoms: Overwhelm, lack of motivation, and difficulty in managing stress. It may also help with feelings of hopelessness and emotional disturbances.

Danburite's homeopathic profile would focus on its ability to cleanse, protect, and elevate, making it suitable for addressing conditions related to emotional healing, energy alignment, and overall health.

Conclusion

Danburite is a vital gemstone in holistic healing, celebrated not just for its beauty but for its versatile healing properties. Whether used for emotional healing, energy balancing, or as a protective talisman, Danburite serves as a potent aid in achieving physical health and spiritual harmony. As with all alternative practices, these should be considered complementary to conventional medical treatments.

Jeremejevite: Comprehensive Guide on Spiritual and Physical Healing Properties

Overview

Jeremejevite, a rare and exquisite gemstone known for its delicate blue hues, is highly valued for its unique energetic properties. This crystal is treasured for its ability to enhance emotional healing, spiritual insight, and overall well-being.

Spiritual and Psychic Benefits

Emotional Healing and Calming: Jeremejevite is highly regarded for its ability to soothe emotional pain and reduce stress. It helps to calm the mind and heart, providing relief from anxiety, sadness, and emotional turmoil.

Spiritual Growth: Associated with the crown and throat chakras, Jeremejevite enhances spiritual awareness and enlightenment. It facilitates a deeper connection to higher realms, promoting inner peace and spiritual growth.

Protection: Jeremejevite is believed to offer protection against negative energies and psychic attacks. It creates a shield of light around the wearer, ensuring a safe and positive energetic environment.

Enhancement of Healing Energies: Known for its high vibrational energy, Jeremejevite amplifies personal energy and enhances the effectiveness of other healing crystals. It is particularly beneficial in energy healing practices for its ability to elevate and harmonize the body's energy fields.

Harmonization and Balance: Jeremejevite assists in balancing the body's subtle energies. It aligns the chakras and stabilizes emotions, fostering a harmonious internal state and promoting overall well-being.

Versatile Use in Healing Practices: Utilized in various forms such as raw crystals, polished stones, and jewelry, Jeremejevite is a key component in holistic healing practices. It is often used in meditation and energy healing sessions to enhance spiritual growth and emotional balance.

Physical Healing Properties

Bone and Joint Health: Jeremejevite is believed to support bone and joint health. It helps with issues related to the skeletal system, promoting overall physical strength and vitality.

Detoxification: This crystal aids in detoxification by supporting the body's natural cleansing processes. It helps to eliminate toxins, promoting overall metabolic health and vitality.

Immune System: Jeremejevite is thought to boost the immune system, helping the body to fight off infections and illnesses more effectively. It supports the body's natural defenses and promotes overall health and vitality.

Energy Balance: By harmonizing the flow of internal energies, Jeremejevite supports physical and emotional health. It helps in the recovery process from various conditions and promotes overall well-being.

Potential Homeopathic Uses

If Jeremejevite were to be used as a homeopathic remedy, its indications might include:

Psychological Symptoms: Mental fatigue, stress, and difficulty in communication. It may also help in cases of emotional instability and trauma.

Physical Symptoms: Bone-related conditions, immune system deficiencies, and metabolic detoxification needs.

Behavioral Symptoms: Overwhelm, lack of motivation, and difficulty in managing stress. It may also help with feelings of hopelessness and emotional disturbances.

Jeremejevite's homeopathic profile would focus on its ability to cleanse, protect, and stabilize, making it suitable for addressing conditions related to mental clarity, energy alignment, and overall health.

Conclusion

Jeremejevite is a vital gemstone in holistic healing, celebrated not just for its beauty but for its versatile healing properties. Whether used for mental clarity, emotional healing, or as a protective talisman, Jeremejevite serves as a potent aid in achieving physical health and spiritual harmony. As with all alternative practices, these should be considered complementary to conventional medical treatments.

Kornerupine: Comprehensive Guide on Spiritual and Physical Healing Properties

Overview

Kornerupine, a unique gemstone known for its green to brown hues, is highly prized for its rarity and powerful energetic properties. This crystal is valued for its ability to enhance mental clarity, emotional healing, and spiritual growth.

Spiritual and Psychic Benefits

Mental Clarity and Focus: Kornerupine is renowned for its ability to enhance mental clarity and focus. It aids in intellectual pursuits and is beneficial for those who need to improve their cognitive abilities.

Spiritual Growth: Associated with the heart and third eye chakras, Kornerupine enhances spiritual awareness and intuition. It facilitates a deeper connection to the higher self and the spiritual realm, promoting spiritual growth and enlightenment.

Emotional Healing: Kornerupine helps to heal emotional wounds and reduce stress. It provides a calming influence, making it easier to manage emotional upheavals and maintain inner peace.

Enhancement of Healing Energies: Known for its high vibrational energy, Kornerupine amplifies personal energy and enhances the effectiveness of other healing crystals. It is particularly beneficial in energy healing practices for its ability to elevate and harmonize the body's energy fields.

Versatile Use in Healing Practices: Utilized in various forms such as raw crystals, polished stones, and jewelry, Kornerupine is a key component in holistic healing practices. It is often used in meditation and energy healing sessions to enhance mental clarity and emotional balance.

Physical Healing Properties

Digestive Health: Kornerupine is believed to support digestive health and improve metabolism. It helps with issues related to the digestive system, promoting overall digestive wellness.

Detoxification: This crystal aids in detoxification by supporting the body's natural cleansing processes. It helps to eliminate toxins, promoting overall metabolic health and vitality.

Immune System: Kornerupine is thought to boost the immune system, helping the body to fight off infections and illnesses more effectively. It supports the body's natural defenses and promotes overall health and vitality.

Energy Balance: By harmonizing the flow of internal energies, Kornerupine supports physical and emotional health. It helps in the recovery process from various conditions and promotes overall well-being.

Potential Homeopathic Uses

If Kornerupine were to be used as a homeopathic remedy, its indications might include:

Psychological Symptoms: Mental fatigue, stress, and difficulty in communication. It may also help in cases of emotional instability and trauma.

Physical Symptoms: Digestive-related conditions, immune system deficiencies, and metabolic detoxification needs.

Behavioral Symptoms: Overwhelm, lack of motivation, and difficulty in managing stress. It may also help with feelings of hopelessness and emotional disturbances.

Kornerupine's homeopathic profile would focus on its ability to cleanse, protect, and stabilize, making it suitable for addressing conditions related to mental clarity, energy alignment, and overall health.

Conclusion

Kornerupine is a vital gemstone in holistic healing, celebrated not just for its beauty but for its versatile healing properties. Whether used for mental clarity, emotional healing, or as a protective talisman, Kornerupine serves as a potent aid in achieving physical health and spiritual harmony. As with all alternative practices, these should be considered complementary to conventional medical treatments.

Petalite: Comprehensive Guide on Spiritual and Physical Healing Properties

Overview

Petalite, known for its gentle pink, white, or colorless hues, is a highly prized gemstone for its calming and protective properties. Often referred to as the "Stone of Angels," Petalite is revered for its ability to connect with higher realms, providing emotional healing and spiritual insight.

Spiritual and Psychic Benefits

Emotional Healing and Calming: Petalite is renowned for its soothing energy, which helps to calm the mind and heart. It alleviates stress, anxiety, and emotional turmoil, promoting inner peace and tranquility.

Spiritual Growth: Associated with the crown and heart chakras, Petalite enhances spiritual awareness and connection to higher realms. It facilitates communication with spirit guides and angels, promoting spiritual growth and enlightenment.

Protection: Petalite is believed to offer strong protective energy, shielding the wearer from negative influences and psychic attacks. It creates a safe and secure energetic environment.

Enhancement of Healing Energies: Known for its gentle yet powerful energy, Petalite amplifies personal energy and enhances the effectiveness of other healing crystals. It is particularly beneficial in energy healing practices for its ability to harmonize and elevate the body's energy fields.

Versatile Use in Healing Practices: Utilized in various forms such as raw crystals, polished stones, and jewelry, Petalite is a key component in holistic healing practices. It is often used in meditation and energy healing sessions to enhance spiritual growth and emotional balance.

Physical Healing Properties

Nervous System: Petalite is believed to support the nervous system, helping to reduce symptoms of anxiety and stress-related conditions. It promotes overall mental health and well-being.

Detoxification: This crystal aids in detoxification by supporting the body's natural cleansing processes. It helps to eliminate toxins, promoting overall metabolic health and vitality.

Immune System: Petalite is thought to boost the immune system, helping the body to fight off infections and illnesses more effectively. It supports the body's natural defenses and promotes overall health and vitality.

Energy Balance: By harmonizing the flow of internal energies, Petalite supports physical and emotional health. It helps in the recovery process from various conditions and promotes overall well-being.

Potential Homeopathic Uses

If Petalite were to be used as a homeopathic remedy, its indications might include:

Psychological Symptoms: Anxiety, stress, and emotional instability. It may also help in cases of emotional trauma and difficulty in managing stress.

Physical Symptoms: Nervous system imbalances, immune system deficiencies, and metabolic detoxification needs.

Behavioral Symptoms: Overwhelm, lack of motivation, and difficulty in managing stress. It may also help with feelings of hopelessness and emotional disturbances.

Petalite's homeopathic profile would focus on its ability to cleanse, protect, and stabilize, making it suitable for addressing conditions related to mental clarity, energy alignment, and overall health.

Conclusion

Petalite is a vital gemstone in holistic healing, celebrated not just for its beauty but for its versatile healing properties. Whether used for emotional healing, energy balancing, or as a protective talisman, Petalite serves as a potent aid in achieving physical health and spiritual harmony. As with all alternative practices, these should be considered complementary to conventional medical treatments.

Poudretteite: Comprehensive Guide on Spiritual and Physical Healing Properties

Overview

Poudretteite, a rare and exquisite gemstone known for its delicate pink to violet hues, is highly valued for its unique energetic properties. This crystal is treasured for its ability to enhance emotional healing, spiritual insight, and overall well-being.

Spiritual and Psychic Benefits

Emotional Healing and Calming: Poudretteite is highly regarded for its ability to soothe emotional pain and reduce stress. It helps to calm the mind and heart, providing relief from anxiety, sadness, and emotional turmoil.

Spiritual Growth: Associated with the heart and crown chakras, Poudretteite enhances spiritual awareness and enlightenment. It facilitates a deeper connection to higher realms, promoting inner peace and spiritual growth.

Protection: Poudretteite is believed to offer protection against negative energies and psychic attacks. It creates a shield of light around the wearer, ensuring a safe and positive energetic environment.

Enhancement of Healing Energies: Known for its high vibrational energy, Poudretteite amplifies personal energy and enhances the effectiveness of other healing crystals. It is particularly beneficial in energy healing practices for its ability to elevate and harmonize the body's energy fields.

Versatile Use in Healing Practices: Utilized in various forms such as raw crystals, polished stones, and jewelry, Poudretteite is a key component in holistic healing practices. It is often used in meditation and energy healing sessions to enhance spiritual growth and emotional balance.

Physical Healing Properties

Heart Health: Poudretteite is believed to support heart health and improve cardiovascular function. It is said to help with heart-related conditions and promote overall heart wellness.

Detoxification: This crystal aids in detoxification by supporting the body's natural cleansing processes. It helps to eliminate toxins, promoting overall metabolic health and vitality.

Immune System: Poudretteite is thought to boost the immune system, helping the body to fight off infections and illnesses more effectively. It supports the body's natural defenses and promotes overall health and vitality.

Energy Balance: By harmonizing the flow of internal energies, Poudretteite supports physical and emotional health. It helps in the recovery process from various conditions and promotes overall well-being.

Potential Homeopathic Uses

If Poudretteite were to be used as a homeopathic remedy, its indications might include:

Psychological Symptoms: Anxiety, emotional stress, and feelings of sadness. It may also help in cases of emotional instability and trauma.

Physical Symptoms: Heart-related conditions, immune system deficiencies, and metabolic detoxification needs.

Behavioral Symptoms: Overwhelm, lack of motivation, and difficulty in managing stress. It may also help with feelings of hopelessness and emotional disturbances.

Poudretteite's homeopathic profile would focus on its ability to cleanse, protect, and elevate, making it suitable for addressing conditions related to emotional healing, energy alignment, and overall health.

Conclusion

Poudretteite is a vital gemstone in holistic healing, celebrated not just for its beauty but for its versatile healing properties. Whether used for emotional healing, energy balancing, or as a protective talisman,

Poudretteite serves as a potent aid in achieving physical health and spiritual harmony. As with all alternative practices, these should be considered complementary to conventional medical treatments.

Scapolite: Comprehensive Guide on Spiritual and Physical Healing Properties

Overview

Scapolite, known for its vibrant yellow, pink, or violet hues, is a gemstone treasured for its transformative and purifying properties. This crystal is highly valued for its ability to enhance personal growth, emotional healing, and spiritual insight.

Spiritual and Psychic Benefits

Emotional Healing and Calming: Scapolite is renowned for its ability to soothe emotional pain and reduce stress. It helps to calm the mind and heart, providing relief from anxiety, sadness, and emotional turmoil.

Spiritual Growth: Associated with the crown and solar plexus chakras, Scapolite enhances spiritual awareness and personal power. It facilitates a deeper connection to higher realms, promoting inner peace and spiritual growth.

Transformation and Purification: Scapolite is believed to aid in personal transformation and the release of negative patterns. It helps to purify the mind and spirit, promoting positive change and spiritual evolution.

Enhancement of Healing Energies: Known for its high vibrational energy, Scapolite amplifies personal energy and enhances the effectiveness of other healing crystals. It is particularly beneficial in energy healing practices for its ability to elevate and harmonize the body's energy fields.

Versatile Use in Healing Practices: Utilized in various forms such as raw crystals, polished stones, and jewelry, Scapolite is a key component in holistic healing practices. It is often used in meditation and energy healing sessions to enhance personal growth and emotional balance.

Physical Healing Properties

Bone and Joint Health: Scapolite is believed to support bone and joint health. It helps with issues related to the skeletal system, promoting overall physical strength and vitality.

Detoxification: This crystal aids in detoxification by supporting the body's natural cleansing processes. It helps to eliminate toxins, promoting overall metabolic health and vitality.

Immune System: Scapolite is thought to boost the immune system, helping the body to fight off infections and illnesses more effectively. It supports the body's natural defenses and promotes overall health and vitality.

Energy Balance: By harmonizing the flow of internal energies, Scapolite supports physical and emotional health. It helps in the recovery process from various conditions and promotes overall well-being.

Potential Homeopathic Uses

If Scapolite were to be used as a homeopathic remedy, its indications might include:

Psychological Symptoms: Anxiety, emotional stress, and feelings of sadness. It may also help in cases of emotional instability and trauma.

Physical Symptoms: Bone-related conditions, immune system deficiencies, and metabolic detoxification needs.

Behavioral Symptoms: Overwhelm, lack of motivation, and difficulty in managing stress. It may also help with feelings of hopelessness and emotional disturbances.

Conclusion

Scapolite is a vital gemstone in holistic healing, celebrated not just for its beauty but for its versatile healing properties. Whether used for emotional healing, energy balancing, or as a transformative aid, Scapolite serves as a potent aid in achieving physical health and spiritual harmony. As with all alternative practices, these should be considered complementary to conventional medical treatments.

Aegirine: Comprehensive Guide on Spiritual and Physical Healing Properties

Overview

Aegirine, with its striking dark green to black needle-like crystals, is a powerful gemstone valued for its energetic and protective qualities. Known for its ability to cleanse and energize, Aegirine is often used in various healing and spiritual practices.

Spiritual and Psychic Benefits

Energy Cleansing and Protection: Aegirine is renowned for its ability to cleanse negative energies from the environment and the aura. It acts as a protective shield, safeguarding against psychic attacks and energy vampires.

Enhancement of Positive Energies: This gemstone amplifies positive energies, fostering a vibrant and uplifting atmosphere. It is particularly useful in transforming negative emotions into positive ones, promoting a sense of joy and optimism.

Spiritual Awakening: Linked to the root and third eye chakras, Aegirine aids in spiritual awakening and development. It enhances intuition and psychic abilities, making it a valuable tool for those on a spiritual journey.

Grounding and Strengthening: Aegirine provides strong grounding energy, helping to anchor and stabilize the user. It strengthens the connection between the physical and spiritual realms, promoting a balanced and centered state of being.

Focus and Determination: This gemstone is known for enhancing focus and determination. It supports the user in overcoming challenges and obstacles, providing the strength and willpower needed to achieve goals.

Physical Healing Properties

Immune System Support: Aegirine is believed to boost the immune system, helping the body to ward off infections and diseases. It supports overall health and enhances the body's natural healing abilities.

Detoxification: This gemstone aids in detoxification processes, helping to cleanse the body of toxins and impurities. It supports liver function and promotes healthy metabolic processes.

Pain Relief and Recovery: Aegirine is known for its pain-relieving properties. It can assist in the recovery from injuries and surgeries, promoting faster healing and reducing discomfort.

Energy Vitalization: Aegirine enhances physical vitality and energy levels. It is particularly beneficial for those experiencing fatigue or low energy, as it helps to invigorate and energize the body.

Respiratory Health: This gemstone supports respiratory health, helping to alleviate symptoms of lung-related conditions. It promotes clear and healthy breathing, making it useful for individuals with respiratory issues.

Potential Homeopathic Uses

If Aegirine were to be used as a homeopathic remedy, its indications might include:

Psychological Symptoms: Stress, anxiety, and emotional imbalance. It may also help in cases of low self-esteem and lack of motivation.

Physical Symptoms: Immune system deficiencies, fatigue, and detoxification needs.

Behavioral Symptoms: Difficulty in focusing, procrastination, and feeling overwhelmed by life's challenges.

Aegirine's homeopathic profile would focus on its ability to cleanse, protect, and energize, making it suitable for addressing conditions related to energy depletion and environmental stress.

Conclusion

Aegirine is a powerful and versatile gemstone, cherished for its protective, cleansing, and energizing properties. Whether used for grounding, enhancing focus, or boosting physical vitality, Aegirine serves as a potent ally in achieving overall well-being and spiritual growth. As with all alternative practices, these should be considered as complementary to conventional medical treatments.

Anatase: Comprehensive Guide on Spiritual and Physical Healing Properties

Overview

Anatase, known for its captivating blue to black hues and unique crystal structure, is a gemstone that holds significant spiritual and healing properties. This gemstone is appreciated for its ability to enhance clarity and focus, making it a valuable tool in both spiritual and physical healing practices.

Spiritual and Psychic Benefits

Clarity and Focus: Anatase is highly regarded for its ability to clear the mind and enhance focus. It helps users to cut through mental fog and achieve a state of clear thinking and concentration.

Spiritual Insight: Linked to the third eye chakra, Anatase promotes spiritual insight and intuitive abilities. It aids in deepening one's spiritual practice and understanding of higher truths.

Energy Alignment: This gemstone helps to align and balance the body's energies, promoting harmony and equilibrium. It supports the alignment of the chakras and the smooth flow of energy throughout the body.

Transformation and Growth: Anatase assists in personal transformation and growth. It encourages letting go of old patterns and embracing new ways of thinking and being.

Protection: Known for its protective qualities, Anatase shields the user from negative energies and psychic attacks. It creates a protective barrier, ensuring a safe and secure environment for spiritual practices.

Physical Healing Properties

Energy Boost: Anatase is believed to provide an energy boost, helping to overcome fatigue and lethargy. It invigorates the body and mind, promoting a sense of vitality and well-being.

Immune Support: This gemstone supports the immune system, enhancing the body's ability to fight off infections and diseases. It promotes overall health and resilience.

Detoxification: Anatase aids in detoxification, helping to cleanse the body of toxins and impurities. It supports liver function and promotes healthy metabolic processes.

Pain Relief: Known for its pain-relieving properties, Anatase can assist in alleviating various types of pain, including headaches and muscle aches. It supports the body's natural healing processes.

Respiratory Health: This gemstone supports respiratory health, helping to clear and strengthen the lungs. It is beneficial for individuals with respiratory issues, promoting clear and healthy breathing.

Potential Homeopathic Uses

If Anatase were to be used as a homeopathic remedy, its indications might include:

Psychological Symptoms: Mental fog, lack of focus, and difficulty concentrating. It may also help with stress and anxiety.

Physical Symptoms: Fatigue, immune deficiencies, and detoxification needs.

Behavioral Symptoms: Procrastination, difficulty in making decisions, and feeling overwhelmed.

Anatase's homeopathic profile would focus on its ability to clear, protect, and energize, making it suitable for addressing conditions related to mental clarity and energy balance.

Conclusion

Anatase is a powerful gemstone, valued for its ability to enhance clarity, focus, and overall well-being. Whether used for spiritual insight, energy alignment, or physical healing, Anatase serves as a potent aid in achieving a balanced and healthy state. As with all alternative practices, these should be considered as complementary to conventional medical treatments.

Andradite: Comprehensive Guide on Spiritual and Physical Healing Properties

Overview

Andradite, a member of the garnet family, is known for its rich colors ranging from green to black. This gemstone is cherished for its potent energy and healing properties, making it a valuable addition to any crystal collection.

Spiritual and Psychic Benefits

Grounding and Stability: Andradite is highly effective for grounding and providing stability. It helps anchor the user to the Earth, promoting a sense of security and balance.

Spiritual Growth: Linked to the root and heart chakras, Andradite facilitates spiritual growth and development. It enhances the connection to higher realms while maintaining a grounded presence.

Energy Amplification: This gemstone is known for its ability to amplify energies. It enhances the power of other crystals and strengthens the overall energy field of the user.

Protection and Shielding: Andradite offers strong protective qualities, shielding the user from negative energies and psychic attacks. It creates a safe space for spiritual practices and meditation.

Courage and Strength: Andradite imbues the user with courage and inner strength. It supports overcoming challenges and facing fears with confidence.

Physical Healing Properties

Vitality and Strength: Andradite is believed to boost physical vitality and strength. It invigorates the body, promoting overall health and energy levels.

Immune Support: This gemstone supports the immune system, enhancing the body's natural defenses. It aids in fighting off infections and diseases, promoting overall well-being.

Detoxification: Andradite aids in detoxification, helping to cleanse the body of toxins and impurities. It supports liver function and promotes healthy metabolic processes.

Bone and Muscle Health: Known for its beneficial effects on the skeletal system, Andradite supports bone and muscle health. It aids in the healing of fractures and injuries.

Circulatory Health: Andradite supports healthy circulation and cardiovascular function. It promotes the flow of blood and oxygen throughout the body, enhancing overall vitality.

Potential Homeopathic Uses

If Andradite were to be used as a homeopathic remedy, its indications might include:

Psychological Symptoms: Anxiety, fear, and lack of confidence. It may also help with feelings of instability and insecurity.

Physical Symptoms: Immune deficiencies, fatigue, and detoxification needs.

Behavioral Symptoms: Difficulty in facing challenges, lack of courage, and feeling overwhelmed.

Andradite's homeopathic profile would focus on its ability to ground, protect, and energize, making it suitable for addressing conditions related to physical vitality and emotional stability.

Conclusion

Andradite is a powerful gemstone, celebrated for its grounding, protective, and energizing properties. Whether used for spiritual growth, physical healing, or enhancing overall well-being, Andradite serves as a potent ally in achieving a balanced and healthy state. As with all alternative practices, these should be considered as complementary to conventional medical treatments.

Axinite: Comprehensive Guide on Spiritual and Physical Healing Properties

Overview

Axinite, with its distinctive brown to violet hues, is a unique gemstone known for its grounding and balancing properties. This crystal is highly valued for its ability to promote harmony and well-being in various aspects of life.

Spiritual and Psychic Benefits

Grounding and Stabilizing: Axinite is renowned for its grounding properties. It helps to stabilize the user's energy and anchor them to the Earth, promoting a sense of security and balance.

Energy Flow and Balance: Linked to the root and sacral chakras, Axinite facilitates the smooth flow of energy throughout the body. It helps to balance and align the chakras, promoting overall energetic harmony.

Connection to Nature: This gemstone enhances the connection to nature and the natural world. It promotes a deep appreciation for the Earth and its energies, fostering a sense of unity with the environment.

Transformation and Growth: Axinite supports personal transformation and growth. It encourages the release of old patterns and the adoption of new, positive ways of thinking and being.

Enhancement of Intuition: Known for its ability to enhance intuition, Axinite aids in developing psychic abilities and deepening one's spiritual practice. It is particularly useful for meditation and introspection.

Physical Healing Properties

Pain Relief and Recovery: Axinite is believed to have pain-relieving properties, helping to alleviate various types of discomfort, including headaches and muscle aches. It supports the body's natural healing processes.

Immune Support: This gemstone supports the immune system, enhancing the body's ability to fight off infections and diseases. It promotes overall health and resilience.

Detoxification: Axinite aids in detoxification, helping to cleanse the body of toxins and impurities. It supports liver function and promotes healthy metabolic processes.

Energy Boost: Known for its energizing properties, Axinite helps to overcome fatigue and lethargy. It invigorates the body and mind, promoting a sense of vitality and well-being.

Bone and Joint Health: Axinite supports bone and joint health, aiding in the healing of fractures and injuries. It promotes overall skeletal strength and flexibility.

Potential Homeopathic Uses

If Axinite were to be used as a homeopathic remedy, its indications might include:

Psychological Symptoms: Anxiety, emotional instability, and stress. It may also help with feelings of disconnection from nature and the environment.

Physical Symptoms: Immune deficiencies, fatigue, and detoxification needs.

Behavioral Symptoms: Difficulty in letting go of old patterns, lack of focus, and feeling overwhelmed.

Axinite's homeopathic profile would focus on its ability to ground, balance, and energize, making it suitable for addressing conditions related to physical vitality and emotional stability.

Conclusion

Axinite is a versatile gemstone, cherished for its grounding, balancing, and energizing properties. Whether used for spiritual growth, physical healing, or enhancing overall well-being, Axinite serves as a potent aid in achieving a balanced and harmonious state. As with all alternative practices, these should be considered as complementary to conventional medical treatments.

Benitoite: Comprehensive Guide on Spiritual and Physical Healing Properties

Overview

Benitoite, known for its stunning blue hues, is a rare and highly sought-after gemstone. This crystal is appreciated for its unique energy and powerful healing properties, making it a valuable tool in various spiritual and physical healing practices.

Spiritual and Psychic Benefits

Spiritual Awakening: Benitoite is highly regarded for its ability to facilitate spiritual awakening and enlightenment. It helps users connect with higher realms and gain deeper insights into their spiritual path.

Intuition and Psychic Abilities: Linked to the third eye chakra, Benitoite enhances intuition and psychic abilities. It aids in developing clairvoyance, telepathy, and other psychic gifts.

Communication and Expression: This gemstone supports clear and effective communication. It helps to articulate thoughts and feelings, promoting honest and open expression.

Calming and Soothing: Benitoite has a calming and soothing energy, helping to alleviate stress and anxiety. It promotes a peaceful state of mind, making it ideal for meditation and relaxation.

Protection and Cleansing: Known for its protective qualities, Benitoite shields the user from negative energies and psychic attacks. It also helps to cleanse and purify the aura, promoting overall energetic health.

Physical Healing Properties

Energy Boost: Benitoite is believed to provide an energy boost, helping to overcome fatigue and lethargy. It invigorates the body and mind, promoting a sense of vitality and well-being.

Immune Support: This gemstone supports the immune system, enhancing the body's natural defenses. It aids in fighting off infections and diseases, promoting overall health.

Detoxification: Benitoite aids in detoxification, helping to cleanse the body of toxins and impurities. It supports liver function and promotes healthy metabolic processes.

Pain Relief: Known for its pain-relieving properties, Benitoite can assist in alleviating various types of pain, including headaches and muscle aches. It supports the body's natural healing processes.

Respiratory Health: This gemstone supports respiratory health, helping to clear and strengthen the lungs. It is beneficial for individuals with respiratory issues, promoting clear and healthy breathing.

Potential Homeopathic Uses

If Benitoite were to be used as a homeopathic remedy, its indications might include:

Psychological Symptoms: Anxiety, stress, and emotional imbalance. It may also help with feelings of isolation and disconnection.

Physical Symptoms: Immune deficiencies, fatigue, and detoxification needs.

Behavioral Symptoms: Difficulty in communicating, lack of focus, and feeling overwhelmed.

Benitoite's homeopathic profile would focus on its ability to calm, protect, and energize, making it suitable for addressing conditions related to emotional balance and energy flow.

Conclusion

Benitoite is a rare and powerful gemstone, valued for its calming, protective, and energizing properties. Whether used for spiritual growth, physical healing, or enhancing overall well-being, Benitoite serves as a potent aid in achieving a balanced and harmonious state. As with all alternative practices, these should be considered as complementary to conventional medical treatments.

Brookite: Comprehensive Guide on Spiritual and Physical Healing Properties

Overview

Brookite, with its distinctive brown to black hues, is a unique and powerful gemstone. This crystal is highly valued for its ability to enhance spiritual awareness and promote physical healing, making it a valuable addition to any crystal collection.

Spiritual and Psychic Benefits

Spiritual Awareness and Growth: Brookite is highly effective in enhancing spiritual awareness and promoting growth. It helps users connect with higher realms and gain deeper insights into their spiritual journey.

Intuition and Psychic Abilities: Linked to the crown and third eye chakras, Brookite enhances intuition and psychic abilities. It aids in developing clairvoyance, telepathy, and other psychic gifts.

Energy Alignment and Balance: This gemstone helps to align and balance the body's energies, promoting harmony and equilibrium. It supports the alignment of the chakras and the smooth flow of energy throughout the body.

Transformation and Change: Brookite supports personal transformation and change. It encourages the release of old patterns and the adoption of new, positive ways of thinking and being.

Protection and Shielding: Known for its protective qualities, Brookite shields the user from negative energies and psychic attacks. It creates a safe space for spiritual practices and meditation.

Physical Healing Properties

Vitality and Strength: Brookite is believed to boost physical vitality and strength. It invigorates the body, promoting overall health and energy levels.

Immune Support: This gemstone supports the immune system, enhancing the body's natural defenses. It aids in fighting off infections and diseases, promoting overall well-being.

Detoxification: Brookite aids in detoxification, helping to cleanse the body of toxins and impurities. It supports liver function and promotes healthy metabolic processes.

Pain Relief: Known for its pain-relieving properties, Brookite can assist in alleviating various types of pain, including headaches and muscle aches. It supports the body's natural healing processes.

Respiratory Health: This gemstone supports respiratory health, helping to clear and strengthen the lungs. It is beneficial for individuals with respiratory issues, promoting clear and healthy breathing.

Potential Homeopathic Uses

If Brookite were to be used as a homeopathic remedy, its indications might include:

Psychological Symptoms: Anxiety, stress, and emotional imbalance. It may also help with feelings of isolation and disconnection.

Physical Symptoms: Immune deficiencies, fatigue, and detoxification needs.

Behavioral Symptoms: Difficulty in letting go of old patterns, lack of focus, and feeling overwhelmed.

Brookite's homeopathic profile would focus on its ability to cleanse, protect, and energize, making it suitable for addressing conditions related to energy flow and emotional stability.

Conclusion

Brookite is a powerful and versatile gemstone, cherished for its grounding, balancing, and energizing properties. Whether used for spiritual growth, physical healing, or enhancing overall well-being, Brookite serves as a potent aid in achieving a balanced and harmonious state. As with all alternative practices, these should be considered as complementary to conventional medical treatments.

Colemanite: Comprehensive Guide on Spiritual and Physical Healing Properties

Overview

Colemanite, known for its translucent white to colorless crystals, is a unique and powerful gemstone. This crystal is highly valued for its ability to enhance spiritual awareness and promote physical healing, making it a valuable addition to any crystal collection.

Spiritual and Psychic Benefits

Spiritual Awareness and Growth: Colemanite is highly effective in enhancing spiritual awareness and promoting growth. It helps users connect with higher realms and gain deeper insights into their spiritual journey.

Intuition and Psychic Abilities: Linked to the crown and third eye chakras, Colemanite enhances intuition and psychic abilities. It aids in developing clairvoyance, telepathy, and other psychic gifts.

Energy Alignment and Balance: This gemstone helps to align and balance the body's energies, promoting harmony and equilibrium. It supports the alignment of the chakras and the smooth flow of energy throughout the body.

Transformation and Change: Colemanite supports personal transformation and change. It encourages the release of old patterns and the adoption of new, positive ways of thinking and being.

Protection and Shielding: Known for its protective qualities, Colemanite shields the user from negative energies and psychic attacks. It creates a safe space for spiritual practices and meditation.

Physical Healing Properties

Vitality and Strength: Colemanite is believed to boost physical vitality and strength. It invigorates the body, promoting overall health and energy levels.

Immune Support: This gemstone supports the immune system, enhancing the body's natural defenses. It aids in fighting off infections and diseases, promoting overall well-being.

Detoxification: Colemanite aids in detoxification, helping to cleanse the body of toxins and impurities. It supports liver function and promotes healthy metabolic processes.

Pain Relief: Known for its pain-relieving properties, Colemanite can assist in alleviating various types of pain, including headaches and muscle aches. It supports the body's natural healing processes.

Respiratory Health: This gemstone supports respiratory health, helping to clear and strengthen the lungs. It is beneficial for individuals with respiratory issues, promoting clear and healthy breathing.

Potential Homeopathic Uses

If Colemanite were to be used as a homeopathic remedy, its indications might include:

Psychological Symptoms: Anxiety, stress, and emotional imbalance. It may also help with feelings of isolation and disconnection.

Physical Symptoms: Immune deficiencies, fatigue, and detoxification needs.

Behavioral Symptoms: Difficulty in letting go of old patterns, lack of focus, and feeling overwhelmed.

Colemanite's homeopathic profile would focus on its ability to cleanse, protect, and energize, making it suitable for addressing conditions related to energy flow and emotional stability.

Conclusion

Colemanite is a powerful and versatile gemstone, cherished for its grounding, balancing, and energizing properties. Whether used for spiritual growth, physical healing, or enhancing overall well-being, Colemanite serves as a potent aid in achieving a balanced and harmonious state. As with all alternative practices, these should be considered as complementary to conventional medical treatments.

Epidote: Comprehensive Guide on Spiritual and Physical Healing Properties

Overview

Epidote, known for its vibrant green hues, is a powerful gemstone appreciated for its healing and transformational properties. This crystal is highly valued for its ability to enhance personal growth and promote physical well-being.

Spiritual and Psychic Benefits

Personal Growth and Transformation: Epidote is highly effective in promoting personal growth and transformation. It helps to release negative patterns and encourages positive change and development.

Emotional Healing: Linked to the heart chakra, Epidote promotes emotional healing and balance. It helps to release emotional blockages and traumas, providing a sense of relief and well-being.

Manifestation and Abundance: This gemstone enhances manifestation abilities and attracts abundance. It supports the realization of goals and desires, promoting prosperity and success.

Protection and Cleansing: Known for its protective qualities, Epidote shields the user from negative energies and psychic attacks. It helps to cleanse and purify the aura, promoting overall energetic health.

Spiritual Growth: Epidote facilitates spiritual growth and development. It enhances the connection to higher realms and deepens one's spiritual practice.

Physical Healing Properties

Immune Support: Epidote supports the immune system, enhancing the body's natural defenses. It aids in fighting off infections and diseases, promoting overall health and resilience.

Detoxification: This gemstone aids in detoxification, helping to cleanse the body of toxins and impurities. It supports liver function and promotes healthy metabolic processes.

Pain Relief: Known for its pain-relieving properties, Epidote can assist in alleviating various types of pain, including headaches and muscle aches. It supports the body's natural healing processes.

Digestive Health: Epidote supports digestive health, helping to alleviate digestive issues and promote healthy digestion. It is beneficial for individuals with digestive problems.

Energy Boost: Epidote provides an energy boost, invigorating the body and mind. It promotes a sense of vitality and enthusiasm, helping to overcome fatigue and lethargy.

Potential Homeopathic Uses

If Epidote were to be used as a homeopathic remedy, its indications might include:

Psychological Symptoms: Anxiety, stress, and emotional imbalance. It may also help with feelings of isolation and disconnection.

Physical Symptoms: Immune deficiencies, fatigue, and detoxification needs.

Behavioral Symptoms: Difficulty in letting go of old patterns, lack of focus, and feeling overwhelmed.

Epidote's homeopathic profile would focus on its ability to cleanse, protect, and energize, making it suitable for addressing conditions related to energy flow and emotional stability.

Conclusion

Epidote is a powerful and versatile gemstone, cherished for its grounding, balancing, and energizing properties. Whether used for spiritual growth, physical healing, or enhancing overall well-being, Epidote serves as a potent aid in achieving a balanced and harmonious state. As with all alternative practices, these should be considered as complementary to conventional medical treatments.

Euclase: Comprehensive Guide on Spiritual and Physical Healing Properties

Overview

Euclase, with its stunning blue to green hues, is a rare and highly sought-after gemstone. This crystal is appreciated for its unique energy and powerful healing properties, making it a valuable tool in various spiritual and physical healing practices.

Spiritual and Psychic Benefits

Spiritual Awakening: Euclase is highly regarded for its ability to facilitate spiritual awakening and enlightenment. It helps users connect with higher realms and gain deeper insights into their spiritual journey.

Intuition and Psychic Abilities: Linked to the throat and third eye chakras, Euclase enhances intuition and psychic abilities. It aids in developing clairvoyance, telepathy, and other psychic gifts.

Communication and Expression: This gemstone supports clear and effective communication. It helps to articulate thoughts and feelings, promoting honest and open expression.

Emotional Healing: Euclase promotes emotional healing and balance. It helps to release emotional blockages and traumas, providing a sense of relief and emotional well-being.

Protection and Cleansing: Known for its protective qualities, Euclase shields the user from negative energies and psychic attacks. It helps to cleanse and purify the aura, promoting overall energetic health.

Physical Healing Properties

Immune Support: Euclase supports the immune system, enhancing the body's natural defenses. It aids in fighting off infections and diseases, promoting overall health and resilience.

Detoxification: This gemstone aids in detoxification, helping to cleanse the body of toxins and impurities. It supports liver function and promotes healthy metabolic processes.

Pain Relief: Known for its pain-relieving properties, Euclase can assist in alleviating various types of pain, including headaches and muscle aches. It supports the body's natural healing processes.

Throat Health: Euclase supports throat health, promoting clear and healthy vocal expression. It helps to alleviate throat-related issues and promotes overall throat function.

Respiratory Health: This gemstone supports respiratory health, helping to clear and strengthen the lungs. It is beneficial for individuals with respiratory issues, promoting clear and healthy breathing.

Potential Homeopathic Uses

If Euclase were to be used as a homeopathic remedy, its indications might include:

Psychological Symptoms: Anxiety, stress, and emotional imbalance. It may also help with feelings of isolation and disconnection.

Physical Symptoms: Immune deficiencies, fatigue, and detoxification needs.

Behavioral Symptoms: Difficulty in communicating, lack of focus, and feeling overwhelmed.

Euclase's homeopathic profile would focus on its ability to cleanse, protect, and energize, making it suitable for addressing conditions related to energy flow and emotional stability.

Conclusion

Euclase is a rare and powerful gemstone, valued for its calming, protective, and energizing properties. Whether used for spiritual growth, physical healing, or enhancing overall well-being, Euclase serves as a potent aid in achieving a balanced and harmonious state. As with all alternative practices, these should be considered as complementary to conventional medical treatments.

Ferberite: Comprehensive Guide on Spiritual and Physical Healing Properties

Overview

Ferberite, known for its dark and dense crystals, is a powerful and grounding gemstone. This crystal is appreciated for its protective and stabilizing properties, making it a valuable tool in various spiritual and physical healing practices.

Spiritual and Psychic Benefits

Grounding and Stability: Ferberite is highly effective in providing grounding and stability. It helps to anchor the user to the Earth, promoting a sense of security and balance.

Protection: Known for its protective qualities, Ferberite shields the user from negative energies and psychic attacks. It creates a safe space for spiritual practices and meditation.

Energy Clearing: This gemstone helps to clear and purify the aura, removing negative energy and emotional blockages. It promotes a healthy and balanced energy field.

Focus and Determination: Ferberite enhances focus and determination. It supports the user in overcoming challenges and achieving their goals with persistence and strength.

Spiritual Growth: Linked to the root chakra, Ferberite facilitates spiritual growth and development. It enhances the connection to higher realms while maintaining a grounded presence.

Physical Healing Properties

Immune Support: Ferberite supports the immune system, enhancing the body's natural defenses. It aids in fighting off infections and diseases, promoting overall health and resilience.

Pain Relief: Known for its pain-relieving properties, Ferberite can assist in alleviating various types of pain, including headaches and muscle aches. It supports the body's natural healing processes.

Detoxification: This gemstone aids in detoxification, helping to cleanse the body of toxins and impurities. It supports liver function and promotes healthy metabolic processes.

Bone and Joint Health: Ferberite supports bone and joint health, aiding in the healing of fractures and injuries. It promotes overall skeletal strength and flexibility.

Energy Boost: Ferberite provides an energy boost, invigorating the body and mind. It promotes a sense of vitality and enthusiasm, helping to overcome fatigue and lethargy.

Potential Homeopathic Uses

If Ferberite were to be used as a homeopathic remedy, its indications might include:

Psychological Symptoms: Anxiety, stress, and emotional imbalance. It may also help with feelings of instability and insecurity.

Physical Symptoms: Immune deficiencies, fatigue, and detoxification needs.

Behavioral Symptoms: Difficulty in focusing, procrastination, and feeling overwhelmed.

Ferberite's homeopathic profile would focus on its ability to ground, protect, and energize, making it suitable for addressing conditions related to physical vitality and emotional stability.

Conclusion

Ferberite is a powerful and versatile gemstone, cherished for its grounding, balancing, and energizing properties. Whether used for spiritual growth, physical healing, or enhancing overall well-being, Ferberite serves as a potent aid in achieving a balanced and harmonious state. As with all alternative practices, these should be considered as complementary to conventional medical treatments.

Ferroaxinite: Comprehensive Guide on Spiritual and Physical Healing Properties

Overview

Ferroaxinite, known for its unique brown to yellow hues, is a powerful gemstone with grounding and healing properties. This crystal is appreciated for its ability to balance energies and promote overall well-being.

Spiritual and Psychic Benefits

Grounding and Stability: Ferroaxinite is highly effective in providing grounding and stability. It helps to anchor the user to the Earth, promoting a sense of security and balance.

Energy Balance: This gemstone helps to balance the body's energies, promoting harmony and equilibrium. It supports the alignment of the chakras and the smooth flow of energy throughout the body.

Emotional Healing: Linked to the root and sacral chakras, Ferroaxinite promotes emotional healing and balance. It helps to release emotional blockages and traumas, providing a sense of relief and well-being.

Focus and Clarity: Ferroaxinite enhances focus and clarity. It supports the user in overcoming mental fog and achieving a state of clear thinking and concentration.

Spiritual Growth: Ferroaxinite facilitates spiritual growth and development. It enhances the connection to higher realms while maintaining a grounded presence.

Physical Healing Properties

Immune Support: Ferroaxinite supports the immune system, enhancing the body's natural defenses. It aids in fighting off infections and diseases, promoting overall health and resilience.

Detoxification: This gemstone aids in detoxification, helping to cleanse the body of toxins and impurities. It supports liver function and promotes healthy metabolic processes.

Pain Relief: Known for its pain-relieving properties, Ferroaxinite can assist in alleviating various types of pain, including headaches and muscle aches. It supports the body's natural healing processes.

Energy Boost: Ferroaxinite provides an energy boost, invigorating the body and mind. It promotes a sense of vitality and enthusiasm, helping to overcome fatigue and lethargy.

Digestive Health: Ferroaxinite supports digestive health, helping to alleviate digestive issues and promote healthy digestion. It is beneficial for individuals with digestive problems.

Potential Homeopathic Uses

If Ferroaxinite were to be used as a homeopathic remedy, its indications might include:

Psychological Symptoms: Anxiety, stress, and emotional imbalance. It may also help with feelings of instability and insecurity.

Physical Symptoms: Immune deficiencies, fatigue, and detoxification needs.

Behavioral Symptoms: Difficulty in focusing, procrastination, and feeling overwhelmed.

Ferroaxinite's homeopathic profile would focus on its ability to ground, balance, and energize, making it suitable for addressing conditions related to physical vitality and emotional stability.

Conclusion

Ferroaxinite is a powerful and versatile gemstone, cherished for its grounding, balancing, and energizing properties. Whether used for spiritual growth, physical healing, or enhancing overall well-being, Ferroaxinite serves as a potent aid in achieving a balanced and harmonious state. As with all alternative practices, these should be considered as complementary to conventional medical treatments.

Fluorapatite: Comprehensive Guide on Spiritual and Physical Healing Properties

Overview

Fluorapatite, with its vibrant green to blue hues, is a unique and powerful gemstone. This crystal is highly valued for its ability to enhance spiritual awareness and promote physical healing, making it a valuable addition to any crystal collection.

Spiritual and Psychic Benefits

Spiritual Awakening: Fluorapatite is highly effective in facilitating spiritual awakening and enlightenment. It helps users connect with higher realms and gain deeper insights into their spiritual journey.

Intuition and Psychic Abilities: Linked to the throat and third eye chakras, Fluorapatite enhances intuition and psychic abilities. It aids in developing clairvoyance, telepathy, and other psychic gifts.

Communication and Expression: This gemstone supports clear and effective communication. It helps to articulate thoughts and feelings, promoting honest and open expression.

Emotional Healing: Fluorapatite promotes emotional healing and balance. It helps to release emotional blockages and traumas, providing a sense of relief and emotional well-being.

Protection and Cleansing: Known for its protective qualities, Fluorapatite shields the user from negative energies and psychic attacks. It helps to cleanse and purify the aura, promoting overall energetic health.

Physical Healing Properties

Immune Support: Fluorapatite supports the immune system, enhancing the body's natural defenses. It aids in fighting off infections and diseases, promoting overall health and resilience.

Detoxification: This gemstone aids in detoxification, helping to cleanse the body of toxins and impurities. It supports liver function and promotes healthy metabolic processes.

Pain Relief: Known for its pain-relieving properties, Fluorapatite can assist in alleviating various types of pain, including headaches and muscle aches. It supports the body's natural healing processes.

Bone and Dental Health: Fluorapatite supports bone and dental health, promoting strong and healthy bones and teeth. It aids in the healing of fractures and dental issues.

Respiratory Health: This gemstone supports respiratory health, helping to clear and strengthen the lungs. It is beneficial for individuals with respiratory issues, promoting clear and healthy breathing.

Potential Homeopathic Uses

If Fluorapatite were to be used as a homeopathic remedy, its indications might include:

Psychological Symptoms: Anxiety, stress, and emotional imbalance. It may also help with feelings of isolation and disconnection.

Physical Symptoms: Immune deficiencies, fatigue, and detoxification needs.

Behavioral Symptoms: Difficulty in communicating, lack of focus, and feeling overwhelmed.

Fluorapatite's homeopathic profile would focus on its ability to cleanse, protect, and energize, making it suitable for addressing conditions related to energy flow and emotional stability.

Conclusion

Fluorapatite is a powerful and versatile gemstone, cherished for its grounding, balancing, and energizing properties. Whether used for spiritual growth, physical healing, or enhancing overall well-being, Fluorapatite serves as a potent aid in achieving a balanced and harmonious state. As with all alternative practices, these should be considered as complementary to conventional medical treatments.

Gehlenite: Comprehensive Guide on Spiritual and Physical Healing Properties

Overview

Gehlenite, with its earthy yellow to green hues, is a unique and powerful gemstone. This crystal is highly valued for its grounding and healing properties, making it a valuable tool in various spiritual and physical healing practices.

Spiritual and Psychic Benefits

Grounding and Stability: Gehlenite is highly effective in providing grounding and stability. It helps to anchor the user to the Earth, promoting a sense of security and balance.

Energy Balance: This gemstone helps to balance the body's energies, promoting harmony and equilibrium. It supports the alignment of the chakras and the smooth flow of energy throughout the body.

Emotional Healing: Linked to the root and sacral chakras, Gehlenite promotes emotional healing and balance. It helps to release emotional blockages and traumas, providing a sense of relief and well-being.

Spiritual Growth: Gehlenite facilitates spiritual growth and development. It enhances the connection to higher realms while maintaining a grounded presence.

Protection and Shielding: Known for its protective qualities, Gehlenite shields the user from negative energies and psychic attacks. It creates a safe space for spiritual practices and meditation.

Physical Healing Properties

Immune Support: Gehlenite supports the immune system, enhancing the body's natural defenses. It aids in fighting off infections and diseases, promoting overall health and resilience.

Detoxification: This gemstone aids in detoxification, helping to cleanse the body of toxins and impurities. It supports liver function and promotes healthy metabolic processes.

Pain Relief: Known for its pain-relieving properties, Gehlenite can assist in alleviating various types of pain, including headaches and muscle aches. It supports the body's natural healing processes.

Bone and Joint Health: Gehlenite supports bone and joint health, aiding in the healing of fractures and injuries. It promotes overall skeletal strength and flexibility.

Energy Boost: Gehlenite provides an energy boost, invigorating the body and mind. It promotes a sense of vitality and enthusiasm, helping to overcome fatigue and lethargy.

Potential Homeopathic Uses

If Gehlenite were to be used as a homeopathic remedy, its indications might include:

Psychological Symptoms: Anxiety, stress, and emotional imbalance. It may also help with feelings of instability and insecurity.

Physical Symptoms: Immune deficiencies, fatigue, and detoxification needs.

Behavioral Symptoms: Difficulty in focusing, procrastination, and feeling overwhelmed.

Gehlenite's homeopathic profile would focus on its ability to ground, balance, and energize, making it suitable for addressing conditions related to physical vitality and emotional stability.

Conclusion

Gehlenite is a powerful and versatile gemstone, cherished for its grounding, balancing, and energizing properties. Whether used for spiritual growth, physical healing, or enhancing overall well-being, Gehlenite serves as a potent aid in achieving a balanced and harmonious state. As with all alternative practices, these should be considered as complementary to conventional medical treatments.

Gibbsite: Comprehensive Guide on Spiritual and Physical Healing Properties

Overview

Gibbsite, known for its translucent to white crystals, is a unique and powerful gemstone. This crystal is highly valued for its calming and healing properties, making it a valuable tool in various spiritual and physical healing practices.

Spiritual and Psychic Benefits

Calming and Soothing: Gibbsite is highly effective in providing a calming and soothing energy. It helps to alleviate stress and anxiety, promoting a peaceful state of mind.

Spiritual Growth: Linked to the crown chakra, Gibbsite facilitates spiritual growth and enlightenment. It enhances the connection to higher realms and deepens one's spiritual practice.

Emotional Healing: This gemstone promotes emotional healing and balance. It helps to release emotional blockages and traumas, providing a sense of relief and well-being.

Protection and Cleansing: Known for its protective qualities, Gibbsite shields the user from negative energies and psychic attacks. It helps to cleanse and purify the aura, promoting overall energetic health.

Focus and Clarity: Gibbsite enhances focus and clarity. It supports the user in overcoming mental fog and achieving a state of clear thinking and concentration.

Physical Healing Properties

Immune Support: Gibbsite supports the immune system, enhancing the body's natural defenses. It aids in fighting off infections and diseases, promoting overall health and resilience.

Detoxification: This gemstone aids in detoxification, helping to cleanse the body of toxins and impurities. It supports liver function and promotes healthy metabolic processes.

Pain Relief: Known for its pain-relieving properties, Gibbsite can assist in alleviating various types of pain, including headaches and muscle aches. It supports the body's natural healing processes.

Respiratory Health: Gibbsite supports respiratory health, helping to clear and strengthen the lungs. It is beneficial for individuals with respiratory issues, promoting clear and healthy breathing.

Energy Boost: Gibbsite provides an energy boost, invigorating the body and mind. It promotes a sense of vitality and enthusiasm, helping to overcome fatigue and lethargy.

Potential Homeopathic Uses

If Gibbsite were to be used as a homeopathic remedy, its indications might include:

Psychological Symptoms: Anxiety, stress, and emotional imbalance. It may also help with feelings of isolation and disconnection.

Physical Symptoms: Immune deficiencies, fatigue, and detoxification needs.

Behavioral Symptoms: Difficulty in focusing, procrastination, and feeling overwhelmed.

Gibbsite's homeopathic profile would focus on its ability to cleanse, protect, and energize, making it suitable for addressing conditions related to energy flow and emotional stability.

Conclusion

Gibbsite is a powerful and versatile gemstone, cherished for its grounding, balancing, and energizing properties. Whether used for spiritual growth, physical healing, or enhancing overall well-being, Gibbsite serves as a potent aid in achieving a balanced and harmonious state. As with all alternative practices, these should be considered as complementary to conventional medical treatments.

Glaucophane: Comprehensive Guide on Spiritual and Physical Healing Properties

Overview

Glaucophane, known for its blue to black hues, is a unique and powerful gemstone. This crystal is highly valued for its calming and grounding properties, making it a valuable tool in various spiritual and physical healing practices.

Spiritual and Psychic Benefits

Calming and Soothing: Glaucophane is highly effective in providing a calming and soothing energy. It helps to alleviate stress and anxiety, promoting a peaceful state of mind.

Spiritual Growth: Linked to the throat and third eye chakras, Glaucophane facilitates spiritual growth and enlightenment. It enhances the connection to higher realms and deepens one's spiritual practice.

Emotional Healing: This gemstone promotes emotional healing and balance. It helps to release emotional blockages and traumas, providing a sense of relief and well-being.

Protection and Cleansing: Known for its protective qualities, Glaucophane shields the user from negative energies and psychic attacks. It helps to cleanse and purify the aura, promoting overall energetic health.

Focus and Clarity: Glaucophane enhances focus and clarity. It supports the user in overcoming mental fog and achieving a state of clear thinking and concentration.

Physical Healing Properties

Immune Support: Glaucophane supports the immune system, enhancing the body's natural defenses. It aids in fighting off infections and diseases, promoting overall health and resilience.

Detoxification: This gemstone aids in detoxification, helping to cleanse the body of toxins and impurities. It supports liver function and promotes healthy metabolic processes.

Pain Relief: Known for its pain-relieving properties, Glaucophane can assist in alleviating various types of pain, including headaches and muscle aches. It supports the body's natural healing processes.

Respiratory Health: Glaucophane supports respiratory health, helping to clear and strengthen the lungs. It is beneficial for individuals with respiratory issues, promoting clear and healthy breathing.

Energy Boost: Glaucophane provides an energy boost, invigorating the body and mind. It promotes a sense of vitality and enthusiasm, helping to overcome fatigue and lethargy.

Potential Homeopathic Uses

If Glaucophane were to be used as a homeopathic remedy, its indications might include:

Psychological Symptoms: Anxiety, stress, and emotional imbalance. It may also help with feelings of isolation and disconnection.

Physical Symptoms: Immune deficiencies, fatigue, and detoxification needs.

Behavioral Symptoms: Difficulty in focusing, procrastination, and feeling overwhelmed.

Glaucophane's homeopathic profile would focus on its ability to cleanse, protect, and energize, making it suitable for addressing conditions related to energy flow and emotional stability.

Conclusion

Glaucophane is a powerful and versatile gemstone, cherished for its grounding, balancing, and energizing properties. Whether used for spiritual growth, physical healing, or enhancing overall well-being, Glaucophane serves as a potent aid in achieving a balanced and harmonious state. As with all alternative practices, these should be considered as complementary to conventional medical treatments.

Helvite: Comprehensive Guide on Spiritual and Physical Healing Properties

Overview

Helvite, known for its striking yellow to brown hues, is a rare and powerful gemstone. This crystal is appreciated for its unique energy and healing properties, making it a valuable tool in various spiritual and physical healing practices.

Spiritual and Psychic Benefits

Spiritual Awakening: Helvite is highly effective in facilitating spiritual awakening and enlightenment. It helps users connect with higher realms and gain deeper insights into their spiritual journey.

Intuition and Psychic Abilities: Linked to the solar plexus and crown chakras, Helvite enhances intuition and psychic abilities. It aids in developing clairvoyance, telepathy, and other psychic gifts.

Energy Boost and Vitality: This gemstone provides an energy boost, invigorating the body and mind. It promotes a sense of vitality and enthusiasm, helping to overcome fatigue and lethargy.

Emotional Healing: Helvite promotes emotional healing and balance. It helps to release emotional blockages and traumas, providing a sense of relief and emotional well-being.

Protection and Cleansing: Known for its protective qualities, Helvite shields the user from negative energies and psychic attacks. It helps to cleanse and purify the aura, promoting overall energetic health.

Physical Healing Properties

Immune Support: Helvite supports the immune system, enhancing the body's natural defenses. It aids in fighting off infections and diseases, promoting overall health and resilience.

Detoxification: This gemstone aids in detoxification, helping to cleanse the body of toxins and impurities. It supports liver function and promotes healthy metabolic processes.

Pain Relief: Known for its pain-relieving properties, Helvite can assist in alleviating various types of pain, including headaches and muscle aches. It supports the body's natural healing processes.

Digestive Health: Helvite supports digestive health, helping to alleviate digestive issues and promote healthy digestion. It is beneficial for individuals with digestive problems.

Respiratory Health: This gemstone supports respiratory health, helping to clear and strengthen the lungs. It is beneficial for individuals with respiratory issues, promoting clear and healthy breathing.

Potential Homeopathic Uses

If Helvite were to be used as a homeopathic remedy, its indications might include:

Psychological Symptoms: Anxiety, stress, and emotional imbalance. It may also help with feelings of isolation and disconnection.

Physical Symptoms: Immune deficiencies, fatigue, and detoxification needs.

Behavioral Symptoms: Difficulty in focusing, procrastination, and feeling overwhelmed.

Helvite's homeopathic profile would focus on its ability to cleanse, protect, and energize, making it suitable for addressing conditions related to energy flow and emotional stability.

Conclusion

Helvite is a powerful and versatile gemstone, cherished for its grounding, balancing, and energizing properties. Whether used for spiritual growth, physical healing, or enhancing overall well-being, Helvite serves as a potent aid in achieving a balanced and harmonious state. As with all alternative practices, these should be considered as complementary to conventional medical treatments.

Huebnerite: Comprehensive Guide on Spiritual and Physical Healing Properties

Overview

Huebnerite, with its striking red to brown hues, is a unique and powerful gemstone. This crystal is highly valued for its grounding and healing properties, making it a valuable tool in various spiritual and physical healing practices.

Spiritual and Psychic Benefits

Grounding and Stability: Huebnerite is highly effective in providing grounding and stability. It helps to anchor the user to the Earth, promoting a sense of security and balance.

Energy Balance: This gemstone helps to balance the body's energies, promoting harmony and equilibrium. It supports the alignment of the chakras and the smooth flow of energy throughout the body.

Emotional Healing: Linked to the root and sacral chakras, Huebnerite promotes emotional healing and balance. It helps to release emotional blockages and traumas, providing a sense of relief and well-being.

Focus and Determination: Huebnerite enhances focus and determination. It supports the user in overcoming challenges and achieving their goals with persistence and strength.

Spiritual Growth: Huebnerite facilitates spiritual growth and development. It enhances the connection to higher realms while maintaining a grounded presence.

Physical Healing Properties

Immune Support: Huebnerite supports the immune system, enhancing the body's natural defenses. It aids in fighting off infections and diseases, promoting overall health and resilience.

Detoxification: This gemstone aids in detoxification, helping to cleanse the body of toxins and impurities. It supports liver function and promotes healthy metabolic processes.

Pain Relief: Known for its pain-relieving properties, Huebnerite can assist in alleviating various types of pain, including headaches and muscle aches. It supports the body's natural healing processes.

Bone and Joint Health: Huebnerite supports bone and joint health, aiding in the healing of fractures and injuries. It promotes overall skeletal strength and flexibility.

Energy Boost: Huebnerite provides an energy boost, invigorating the body and mind. It promotes a sense of vitality and enthusiasm, helping to overcome fatigue and lethargy.

Potential Homeopathic Uses

If Huebnerite were to be used as a homeopathic remedy, its indications might include:

Psychological Symptoms: Anxiety, stress, and emotional imbalance. It may also help with feelings of instability and insecurity.

Physical Symptoms: Immune deficiencies, fatigue, and detoxification needs.

Behavioral Symptoms: Difficulty in focusing, procrastination, and feeling overwhelmed.

Huebnerite's homeopathic profile would focus on its ability to ground, balance, and energize, making it suitable for addressing conditions related to physical vitality and emotional stability.

Conclusion

Huebnerite is a powerful and versatile gemstone, cherished for its grounding, balancing, and energizing properties. Whether used for spiritual growth, physical healing, or enhancing overall well-being, Huebnerite serves as a potent aid in achieving a balanced and harmonious state. As with all alternative practices, these should be considered as complementary to conventional medical treatments.

Kammererite: Comprehensive Guide on Spiritual and Physical Healing Properties

Overview

Kammererite, known for its striking purple hues, is a unique and powerful gemstone. This crystal is highly valued for its ability to enhance spiritual awareness and promote physical healing, making it a valuable addition to any crystal collection.

Spiritual and Psychic Benefits

Spiritual Awakening: Kammererite is highly effective in facilitating spiritual awakening and enlightenment. It helps users connect with higher realms and gain deeper insights into their spiritual journey.

Intuition and Psychic Abilities: Linked to the crown and third eye chakras, Kammererite enhances intuition and psychic abilities. It aids in developing clairvoyance, telepathy, and other psychic gifts.

Emotional Healing: Kammererite promotes emotional healing and balance. It helps to release emotional blockages and traumas, providing a sense of relief and well-being.

Protection and Cleansing: Known for its protective qualities, Kammererite shields the user from negative energies and psychic attacks. It helps to cleanse and purify the aura, promoting overall energetic health.

Focus and Clarity: Kammererite enhances focus and clarity. It supports the user in overcoming mental fog and achieving a state of clear thinking and concentration.

Physical Healing Properties

Immune Support: Kammererite supports the immune system, enhancing the body's natural defenses. It aids in fighting off infections and diseases, promoting overall health and resilience.

Detoxification: This gemstone aids in detoxification, helping to cleanse the body of toxins and impurities. It supports liver function and promotes healthy metabolic processes.

Pain Relief: Known for its pain-relieving properties, Kammererite can assist in alleviating various types of pain, including headaches and muscle aches. It supports the body's natural healing processes.

Respiratory Health: Kammererite supports respiratory health, helping to clear and strengthen the lungs. It is beneficial for individuals with respiratory issues, promoting clear and healthy breathing.

Energy Boost: Kammererite provides an energy boost, invigorating the body and mind. It promotes a sense of vitality and enthusiasm, helping to overcome fatigue and lethargy.

Potential Homeopathic Uses

If Kammererite were to be used as a homeopathic remedy, its indications might include:

Psychological Symptoms: Anxiety, stress, and emotional imbalance. It may also help with feelings of isolation and disconnection.

Physical Symptoms: Immune deficiencies, fatigue, and detoxification needs.

Behavioral Symptoms: Difficulty in focusing, procrastination, and feeling overwhelmed.

Kammererite's homeopathic profile would focus on its ability to cleanse, protect, and energize, making it suitable for addressing conditions related to energy flow and emotional stability.

Conclusion

Kammererite is a powerful and versatile gemstone, cherished for its grounding, balancing, and energizing properties. Whether used for spiritual growth, physical healing, or enhancing overall well-being, Kammererite serves as a potent aid in achieving a balanced and harmonious state. As with all alternative practices, these should be considered as complementary to conventional medical treatments.

Leucite: Comprehensive Guide on Spiritual and Physical Healing Properties

Overview

Leucite, known for its white to gray hues, is a unique and powerful gemstone. This crystal is highly valued for its grounding and healing properties, making it a valuable tool in various spiritual and physical healing practices.

Spiritual and Psychic Benefits

Grounding and Stability: Leucite is highly effective in providing grounding and stability. It helps to anchor the user to the Earth, promoting a sense of security and balance.

Energy Balance: This gemstone helps to balance the body's energies, promoting harmony and equilibrium. It supports the alignment of the chakras and the smooth flow of energy throughout the body.

Emotional Healing: Linked to the root chakra, Leucite promotes emotional healing and balance. It helps to release emotional blockages and traumas, providing a sense of relief and well-being.

Spiritual Growth: Leucite facilitates spiritual growth and development. It enhances the connection to higher realms while maintaining a grounded presence.

Protection and Shielding: Known for its protective qualities, Leucite shields the user from negative energies and psychic attacks. It creates a safe space for spiritual practices and meditation.

Physical Healing Properties

Immune Support: Leucite supports the immune system, enhancing the body's natural defenses. It aids in fighting off infections and diseases, promoting overall health and resilience.

Detoxification: This gemstone aids in detoxification, helping to cleanse the body of toxins and impurities. It supports liver function and promotes healthy metabolic processes.

Pain Relief: Known for its pain-relieving properties, Leucite can assist in alleviating various types of pain, including headaches and muscle aches. It supports the body's natural healing processes.

Bone and Joint Health: Leucite supports bone and joint health, aiding in the healing of fractures and injuries. It promotes overall skeletal strength and flexibility.

Energy Boost: Leucite provides an energy boost, invigorating the body and mind. It promotes a sense of vitality and enthusiasm, helping to overcome fatigue and lethargy.

Potential Homeopathic Uses

If Leucite were to be used as a homeopathic remedy, its indications might include:

Psychological Symptoms: Anxiety, stress, and emotional imbalance. It may also help with feelings of instability and insecurity.

Physical Symptoms: Immune deficiencies, fatigue, and detoxification needs.

Behavioral Symptoms: Difficulty in focusing, procrastination, and feeling overwhelmed.

Leucite's homeopathic profile would focus on its ability to ground, balance, and energize, making it suitable for addressing conditions related to physical vitality and emotional stability.

Conclusion

Leucite is a powerful and versatile gemstone, cherished for its grounding, balancing, and energizing properties. Whether used for spiritual growth, physical healing, or enhancing overall well-being, Leucite serves as a potent aid in achieving a balanced and harmonious state. As with all alternative practices, these should be considered as complementary to conventional medical treatments.

Natrolite: Comprehensive Guide on Spiritual and Physical Healing Properties

Overview

Natrolite, known for its white to colorless crystal formations, is a unique and powerful gemstone. This crystal is highly valued for its purifying and energizing properties, making it a valuable tool in various spiritual and physical healing practices.

Spiritual and Psychic Benefits

Spiritual Awakening: Natrolite is highly effective in facilitating spiritual awakening and enlightenment. It helps users connect with higher realms and gain deeper insights into their spiritual journey.

Intuition and Psychic Abilities: Linked to the crown and third eye chakras, Natrolite enhances intuition and psychic abilities. It aids in developing clairvoyance, telepathy, and other psychic gifts.

Energy Clearing: This gemstone helps to clear and purify the aura, removing negative energy and emotional blockages. It promotes a healthy and balanced energy field.

Protection and Cleansing: Known for its protective qualities, Natrolite shields the user from negative energies and psychic attacks. It helps to cleanse and purify the aura, promoting overall energetic health.

Focus and Clarity: Natrolite enhances focus and clarity. It supports the user in overcoming mental fog and achieving a state of clear thinking and concentration.

Physical Healing Properties

Immune Support: Natrolite supports the immune system, enhancing the body's natural defenses. It aids in fighting off infections and diseases, promoting overall health and resilience.

Detoxification: This gemstone aids in detoxification, helping to cleanse the body of toxins and impurities. It supports liver function and promotes healthy metabolic processes.

Pain Relief: Known for its pain-relieving properties, Natrolite can assist in alleviating various types of pain, including headaches and muscle aches. It supports the body's natural healing processes.

Bone and Joint Health: Natrolite supports bone and joint health, aiding in the healing of fractures and injuries. It promotes overall skeletal strength and flexibility.

Respiratory Health: This gemstone supports respiratory health, helping to clear and strengthen the lungs. It is beneficial for individuals with respiratory issues, promoting clear and healthy breathing.

Potential Homeopathic Uses

If Natrolite were to be used as a homeopathic remedy, its indications might include:

Psychological Symptoms: Anxiety, stress, and emotional imbalance. It may also help with feelings of isolation and disconnection.

Physical Symptoms: Immune deficiencies, fatigue, and detoxification needs.

Behavioral Symptoms: Difficulty in focusing, procrastination, and feeling overwhelmed.

Natrolite's homeopathic profile would focus on its ability to cleanse, protect, and energize, making it suitable for addressing conditions related to energy flow and emotional stability.

Conclusion

Natrolite is a powerful and versatile gemstone, cherished for its grounding, balancing, and energizing properties. Whether used for spiritual growth, physical healing, or enhancing overall well-being, Natrolite serves as a potent aid in achieving a balanced and harmonious state. As with all alternative practices, these should be considered as complementary to conventional medical treatments.

Neptunite: Comprehensive Guide on Spiritual and Physical Healing Properties

Overview

Neptunite, with its deep black to reddish-brown hues, is a unique and powerful gemstone. This crystal is highly valued for its grounding and protective properties, making it a valuable tool in various spiritual and physical healing practices.

Spiritual and Psychic Benefits

Grounding and Stability: Neptunite is highly effective in providing grounding and stability. It helps to anchor the user to the Earth, promoting a sense of security and balance.

Protection: Known for its protective qualities, Neptunite shields the user from negative energies and psychic attacks. It creates a safe space for spiritual practices and meditation.

Energy Balance: This gemstone helps to balance the body's energies, promoting harmony and equilibrium. It supports the alignment of the chakras and the smooth flow of energy throughout the body.

Emotional Healing: Linked to the root and sacral chakras, Neptunite promotes emotional healing and balance. It helps to release emotional blockages and traumas, providing a sense of relief and well-being.

Focus and Determination: Neptunite enhances focus and determination. It supports the user in overcoming challenges and achieving their goals with persistence and strength.

Physical Healing Properties

Immune Support: Neptunite supports the immune system, enhancing the body's natural defenses. It aids in fighting off infections and diseases, promoting overall health and resilience.

Detoxification: This gemstone aids in detoxification, helping to cleanse the body of toxins and impurities. It supports liver function and promotes healthy metabolic processes.

Pain Relief: Known for its pain-relieving properties, Neptunite can assist in alleviating various types of pain, including headaches and muscle aches. It supports the body's natural healing processes.

Bone and Joint Health: Neptunite supports bone and joint health, aiding in the healing of fractures and injuries. It promotes overall skeletal strength and flexibility.

Energy Boost: Neptunite provides an energy boost, invigorating the body and mind. It promotes a sense of vitality and enthusiasm, helping to overcome fatigue and lethargy.

Potential Homeopathic Uses

If Neptunite were to be used as a homeopathic remedy, its indications might include:

Psychological Symptoms: Anxiety, stress, and emotional imbalance. It may also help with feelings of instability and insecurity.

Physical Symptoms: Immune deficiencies, fatigue, and detoxification needs.

Behavioral Symptoms: Difficulty in focusing, procrastination, and feeling overwhelmed.

Neptunite's homeopathic profile would focus on its ability to ground, balance, and energize, making it suitable for addressing conditions related to physical vitality and emotional stability.

Conclusion

Neptunite is a powerful and versatile gemstone, cherished for its grounding, balancing, and energizing properties. Whether used for spiritual growth, physical healing, or enhancing overall well-being, Neptunite serves as a potent aid in achieving a balanced and harmonious state. As with all alternative practices, these should be considered as complementary to conventional medical treatments.

Parisite: Comprehensive Guide on Spiritual and Physical Healing Properties

Overview

Parisite, known for its brown to yellowish hues, is a rare and powerful gemstone. This crystal is appreciated for its unique energy and healing properties, making it a valuable tool in various spiritual and physical healing practices.

Spiritual and Psychic Benefits

Spiritual Awakening: Parisite is highly effective in facilitating spiritual awakening and enlightenment. It helps users connect with higher realms and gain deeper insights into their spiritual journey.

Intuition and Psychic Abilities: Linked to the third eye and crown chakras, Parisite enhances intuition and psychic abilities. It aids in developing clairvoyance, telepathy, and other psychic gifts.

Energy Clearing: This gemstone helps to clear and purify the aura, removing negative energy and emotional blockages. It promotes a healthy and balanced energy field.

Protection and Cleansing: Known for its protective qualities, Parisite shields the user from negative energies and psychic attacks. It helps to cleanse and purify the aura, promoting overall energetic health.

Focus and Clarity: Parisite enhances focus and clarity. It supports the user in overcoming mental fog and achieving a state of clear thinking and concentration.

Physical Healing Properties

Immune Support: Parisite supports the immune system, enhancing the body's natural defenses. It aids in fighting off infections and diseases, promoting overall health and resilience.

Detoxification: This gemstone aids in detoxification, helping to cleanse the body of toxins and impurities. It supports liver function and promotes healthy metabolic processes.

Pain Relief: Known for its pain-relieving properties, Parisite can assist in alleviating various types of pain, including headaches and muscle aches. It supports the body's natural healing processes.

Bone and Joint Health: Parisite supports bone and joint health, aiding in the healing of fractures and injuries. It promotes overall skeletal strength and flexibility.

Respiratory Health: This gemstone supports respiratory health, helping to clear and strengthen the lungs. It is beneficial for individuals with respiratory issues, promoting clear and healthy breathing.

Potential Homeopathic Uses

If Parisite were to be used as a homeopathic remedy, its indications might include:

Psychological Symptoms: Anxiety, stress, and emotional imbalance. It may also help with feelings of isolation and disconnection.

Physical Symptoms: Immune deficiencies, fatigue, and detoxification needs.

Behavioral Symptoms: Difficulty in focusing, procrastination, and feeling overwhelmed.

Parisite's homeopathic profile would focus on its ability to cleanse, protect, and energize, making it suitable for addressing conditions related to energy flow and emotional stability.

Conclusion

Parisite is a powerful and versatile gemstone, cherished for its grounding, balancing, and energizing properties. Whether used for spiritual growth, physical healing, or enhancing overall well-being, Parisite serves as a potent aid in achieving a balanced and harmonious state. As with all alternative practices, these should be considered as complementary to conventional medical treatments.

Pericline: Comprehensive Guide on Spiritual and Physical Healing Properties

Overview

Pericline, known for its white to light-colored hues, is a unique and powerful gemstone. This crystal is highly valued for its calming and healing properties, making it a valuable tool in various spiritual and physical healing practices.

Spiritual and Psychic Benefits

Calming and Soothing: Pericline is highly effective in providing a calming and soothing energy. It helps to alleviate stress and anxiety, promoting a peaceful state of mind.

Spiritual Growth: Linked to the crown and third eye chakras, Pericline facilitates spiritual growth and enlightenment. It enhances the connection to higher realms and deepens one's spiritual practice.

Emotional Healing: This gemstone promotes emotional healing and balance. It helps to release emotional blockages and traumas, providing a sense of relief and well-being.

Protection and Cleansing: Known for its protective qualities, Pericline shields the user from negative energies and psychic attacks. It helps to cleanse and purify the aura, promoting overall energetic health.

Focus and Clarity: Pericline enhances focus and clarity. It supports the user in overcoming mental fog and achieving a state of clear thinking and concentration.

Physical Healing Properties

Immune Support: Pericline supports the immune system, enhancing the body's natural defenses. It aids in fighting off infections and diseases, promoting overall health and resilience.

Detoxification: This gemstone aids in detoxification, helping to cleanse the body of toxins and impurities. It supports liver function and promotes healthy metabolic processes.

Pain Relief: Known for its pain-relieving properties, Pericline can assist in alleviating various types of pain, including headaches and muscle aches. It supports the body's natural healing processes.

Respiratory Health: Pericline supports respiratory health, helping to clear and strengthen the lungs. It is beneficial for individuals with respiratory issues, promoting clear and healthy breathing.

Energy Boost: Pericline provides an energy boost, invigorating the body and mind. It promotes a sense of vitality and enthusiasm, helping to overcome fatigue and lethargy.

Potential Homeopathic Uses

If Pericline were to be used as a homeopathic remedy, its indications might include:

Psychological Symptoms: Anxiety, stress, and emotional imbalance. It may also help with feelings of isolation and disconnection.

Physical Symptoms: Immune deficiencies, fatigue, and detoxification needs.

Behavioral Symptoms: Difficulty in focusing, procrastination, and feeling overwhelmed.

Pericline's homeopathic profile would focus on its ability to cleanse, protect, and energize, making it suitable for addressing conditions related to energy flow and emotional stability.

Conclusion

Pericline is a powerful and versatile gemstone, cherished for its grounding, balancing, and energizing properties. Whether used for spiritual growth, physical healing, or enhancing overall well-being, Pericline serves as a potent aid in achieving a balanced and harmonious state. As with all alternative practices, these should be considered as complementary to conventional medical treatments.

Proustite: Comprehensive Guide on Spiritual and Physical Healing Properties

Overview

Proustite, with its striking red hues, is a unique and powerful gemstone. This crystal is highly valued for its grounding and healing properties, making it a valuable tool in various spiritual and physical healing practices.

Spiritual and Psychic Benefits

Grounding and Stability: Proustite is highly effective in providing grounding and stability. It helps to anchor the user to the Earth, promoting a sense of security and balance.

Energy Balance: This gemstone helps to balance the body's energies, promoting harmony and equilibrium. It supports the alignment of the chakras and the smooth flow of energy throughout the body.

Emotional Healing: Linked to the root and sacral chakras, Proustite promotes emotional healing and balance. It helps to release emotional blockages and traumas, providing a sense of relief and well-being.

Focus and Determination: Proustite enhances focus and determination. It supports the user in overcoming challenges and achieving their goals with persistence and strength.

Spiritual Growth: Proustite facilitates spiritual growth and development. It enhances the connection to higher realms while maintaining a grounded presence.

Physical Healing Properties

Immune Support: Proustite supports the immune system, enhancing the body's natural defenses. It aids in fighting off infections and diseases, promoting overall health and resilience.

Detoxification: This gemstone aids in detoxification, helping to cleanse the body of toxins and impurities. It supports liver function and promotes healthy metabolic processes.

Pain Relief: Known for its pain-relieving properties, Proustite can assist in alleviating various types of pain, including headaches and muscle aches. It supports the body's natural healing processes.

Bone and Joint Health: Proustite supports bone and joint health, aiding in the healing of fractures and injuries. It promotes overall skeletal strength and flexibility.

Energy Boost: Proustite provides an energy boost, invigorating the body and mind. It promotes a sense of vitality and enthusiasm, helping to overcome fatigue and lethargy.

Potential Homeopathic Uses

If Proustite were to be used as a homeopathic remedy, its indications might include:

Psychological Symptoms: Anxiety, stress, and emotional imbalance. It may also help with feelings of instability and insecurity.

Physical Symptoms: Immune deficiencies, fatigue, and detoxification needs.

Behavioral Symptoms: Difficulty in focusing, procrastination, and feeling overwhelmed.

Proustite's homeopathic profile would focus on its ability to ground, balance, and energize, making it suitable for addressing conditions related to physical vitality and emotional stability.

Conclusion

Proustite is a powerful and versatile gemstone, cherished for its grounding, balancing, and energizing properties. Whether used for spiritual growth, physical healing, or enhancing overall well-being, Proustite serves as a potent aid in achieving a balanced and harmonious state. As with all alternative practices, these should be considered as complementary to conventional medical treatments.

Pyromorphite: Comprehensive Guide on Spiritual and Physical Healing Properties

Overview

Pyromorphite, known for its vibrant green to brown hues, is a unique and powerful gemstone. This crystal is highly valued for its energizing and healing properties, making it a valuable tool in various spiritual and physical healing practices.

Spiritual and Psychic Benefits

Energy Boost and Vitality: Pyromorphite is highly effective in providing an energy boost. It invigorates the body and mind, promoting a sense of vitality and enthusiasm.

Spiritual Growth: Linked to the heart and solar plexus chakras, Pyromorphite facilitates spiritual growth and enlightenment. It enhances the connection to higher realms and deepens one's spiritual practice.

Emotional Healing: This gemstone promotes emotional healing and balance. It helps to release emotional blockages and traumas, providing a sense of relief and well-being.

Protection and Cleansing: Known for its protective qualities, Pyromorphite shields the user from negative energies and psychic attacks. It helps to cleanse and purify the aura, promoting overall energetic health.

Focus and Clarity: Pyromorphite enhances focus and clarity. It supports the user in overcoming mental fog and achieving a state of clear thinking and concentration.

Physical Healing Properties

Immune Support: Pyromorphite supports the immune system, enhancing the body's natural defenses. It aids in fighting off infections and diseases, promoting overall health and resilience.

Detoxification: This gemstone aids in detoxification, helping to cleanse the body of toxins and impurities. It supports liver function and promotes healthy metabolic processes.

Pain Relief: Known for its pain-relieving properties, Pyromorphite can assist in alleviating various types of pain, including headaches and muscle aches. It supports the body's natural healing processes.

Respiratory Health: Pyromorphite supports respiratory health, helping to clear and strengthen the lungs. It is beneficial for individuals with respiratory issues, promoting clear and healthy breathing.

Bone and Joint Health: Pyromorphite supports bone and joint health, aiding in the healing of fractures and injuries. It promotes overall skeletal strength and flexibility.

Potential Homeopathic Uses

If Pyromorphite were to be used as a homeopathic remedy, its indications might include:

Psychological Symptoms: Anxiety, stress, and emotional imbalance. It may also help with feelings of isolation and disconnection.

Physical Symptoms: Immune deficiencies, fatigue, and detoxification needs.

Behavioral Symptoms: Difficulty in focusing, procrastination, and feeling overwhelmed.

Pyromorphite's homeopathic profile would focus on its ability to cleanse, protect, and energize, making it suitable for addressing conditions related to energy flow and emotional stability.

Conclusion

Pyromorphite is a powerful and versatile gemstone, cherished for its grounding, balancing, and energizing properties. Whether used for spiritual growth, physical healing, or enhancing overall well-being, Pyromorphite serves as a potent aid in achieving a balanced and harmonious state. As with all alternative practices, these should be considered as complementary to conventional medical treatments.

Scheelite: Comprehensive Guide on Spiritual and Physical Healing Properties

Overview

Scheelite, known for its vibrant orange to yellow hues, is a unique and powerful gemstone. This crystal is highly valued for its energizing and healing properties, making it a valuable tool in various spiritual and physical healing practices.

Spiritual and Psychic Benefits

Energy Boost and Vitality: Scheelite is highly effective in providing an energy boost. It invigorates the body and mind, promoting a sense of vitality and enthusiasm.

Spiritual Growth: Linked to the solar plexus and sacral chakras, Scheelite facilitates spiritual growth and enlightenment. It enhances the connection to higher realms and deepens one's spiritual practice.

Emotional Healing: This gemstone promotes emotional healing and balance. It helps to release emotional blockages and traumas, providing a sense of relief and well-being.

Protection and Cleansing: Known for its protective qualities, Scheelite shields the user from negative energies and psychic attacks. It helps to cleanse and purify the aura, promoting overall energetic health.

Focus and Clarity: Scheelite enhances focus and clarity. It supports the user in overcoming mental fog and achieving a state of clear thinking and concentration.

Physical Healing Properties

Immune Support: Scheelite supports the immune system, enhancing the body's natural defenses. It aids in fighting off infections and diseases, promoting overall health and resilience.

Detoxification: This gemstone aids in detoxification, helping to cleanse the body of toxins and impurities. It supports liver function and promotes healthy metabolic processes.

Pain Relief: Known for its pain-relieving properties, Scheelite can assist in alleviating various types of pain, including headaches and muscle aches. It supports the body's natural healing processes.

Respiratory Health: Scheelite supports respiratory health, helping to clear and strengthen the lungs. It is beneficial for individuals with respiratory issues, promoting clear and healthy breathing.

Bone and Joint Health: Scheelite supports bone and joint health, aiding in the healing of fractures and injuries. It promotes overall skeletal strength and flexibility.

Potential Homeopathic Uses

If Scheelite were to be used as a homeopathic remedy, its indications might include:

Psychological Symptoms: Anxiety, stress, and emotional imbalance. It may also help with feelings of isolation and disconnection.

Physical Symptoms: Immune deficiencies, fatigue, and detoxification needs.

Behavioral Symptoms: Difficulty in focusing, procrastination, and feeling overwhelmed.

Scheelite's homeopathic profile would focus on its ability to cleanse, protect, and energize, making it suitable for addressing conditions related to energy flow and emotional stability.

Conclusion

Scheelite is a powerful and versatile gemstone, cherished for its grounding, balancing, and energizing properties. Whether used for spiritual growth, physical healing, or enhancing overall well-being, Scheelite serves as a potent aid in achieving a balanced and harmonious state. As with all alternative practices, these should be considered as complementary to conventional medical treatments.

Tennantite: Comprehensive Guide on Spiritual and Physical Healing Properties

Overview

Tennantite, known for its metallic gray to black hues, is a unique and powerful gemstone. This crystal is highly valued for its grounding and protective properties, making it a valuable tool in various spiritual and physical healing practices.

Spiritual and Psychic Benefits

Grounding and Stability: Tennantite is highly effective in providing grounding and stability. It helps to anchor the user to the Earth, promoting a sense of security and balance.

Protection: Known for its protective qualities, Tennantite shields the user from negative energies and psychic attacks. It creates a safe space for spiritual practices and meditation.

Energy Balance: This gemstone helps to balance the body's energies, promoting harmony and equilibrium. It supports the alignment of the chakras and the smooth flow of energy throughout the body.

Emotional Healing: Linked to the root chakra, Tennantite promotes emotional healing and balance. It helps to release emotional blockages and traumas, providing a sense of relief and well-being.

Focus and Determination: Tennantite enhances focus and determination. It supports the user in overcoming challenges and achieving their goals with persistence and strength.

Physical Healing Properties

Immune Support: Tennantite supports the immune system, enhancing the body's natural defenses. It aids in fighting off infections and diseases, promoting overall health and resilience.

Detoxification: This gemstone aids in detoxification, helping to cleanse the body of toxins and impurities. It supports liver function and promotes healthy metabolic processes.

Pain Relief: Known for its pain-relieving properties, Tennantite can assist in alleviating various types of pain, including headaches and muscle aches. It supports the body's natural healing processes.

Bone and Joint Health: Tennantite supports bone and joint health, aiding in the healing of fractures and injuries. It promotes overall skeletal strength and flexibility.

Energy Boost: Tennantite provides an energy boost, invigorating the body and mind. It promotes a sense of vitality and enthusiasm, helping to overcome fatigue and lethargy.

Potential Homeopathic Uses

If Tennantite were to be used as a homeopathic remedy, its indications might include:

Psychological Symptoms: Anxiety, stress, and emotional imbalance. It may also help with feelings of instability and insecurity.

Physical Symptoms: Immune deficiencies, fatigue, and detoxification needs.

Behavioral Symptoms: Difficulty in focusing, procrastination, and feeling overwhelmed.

Tennantite's homeopathic profile would focus on its ability to ground, balance, and energize, making it suitable for addressing conditions related to physical vitality and emotional stability.

Conclusion

Tennantite is a powerful and versatile gemstone, cherished for its grounding, balancing, and energizing properties. Whether used for spiritual growth, physical healing, or enhancing overall well-being, Tennantite serves as a potent aid in achieving a balanced and harmonious state. As with all alternative practices, these should be considered as complementary to conventional medical treatments.

Wurtzite: Comprehensive Guide on Spiritual and Physical Healing Properties

Overview

Wurtzite, with its brown to black hues, is a unique and powerful gemstone. This crystal is highly valued for its grounding and protective properties, making it a valuable tool in various spiritual and physical healing practices.

Spiritual and Psychic Benefits

Grounding and Stability: Wurtzite is highly effective in providing grounding and stability. It helps to anchor the user to the Earth, promoting a sense of security and balance.

Protection: Known for its protective qualities, Wurtzite shields the user from negative energies and psychic attacks. It creates a safe space for spiritual practices and meditation.

Energy Balance: This gemstone helps to balance the body's energies, promoting harmony and equilibrium. It supports the alignment of the chakras and the smooth flow of energy throughout the body.

Emotional Healing: Linked to the root chakra, Wurtzite promotes emotional healing and balance. It helps to release emotional blockages and traumas, providing a sense of relief and well-being.

Focus and Determination: Wurtzite enhances focus and determination. It supports the user in overcoming challenges and achieving their goals with persistence and strength.

Physical Healing Properties

Immune Support: Wurtzite supports the immune system, enhancing the body's natural defenses. It aids in fighting off infections and diseases, promoting overall health and resilience.

Detoxification: This gemstone aids in detoxification, helping to cleanse the body of toxins and impurities. It supports liver function and promotes healthy metabolic processes.

Pain Relief: Known for its pain-relieving properties, Wurtzite can assist in alleviating various types of pain, including headaches and muscle aches. It supports the body's natural healing processes.

Bone and Joint Health: Wurtzite supports bone and joint health, aiding in the healing of fractures and injuries. It promotes overall skeletal strength and flexibility.

Energy Boost: Wurtzite provides an energy boost, invigorating the body and mind. It promotes a sense of vitality and enthusiasm, helping to overcome fatigue and lethargy.

Potential Homeopathic Uses

If Wurtzite were to be used as a homeopathic remedy, its indications might include:

Psychological Symptoms: Anxiety, stress, and emotional imbalance. It may also help with feelings of instability and insecurity.

Physical Symptoms: Immune deficiencies, fatigue, and detoxification needs.

Behavioral Symptoms: Difficulty in focusing, procrastination, and feeling overwhelmed.

Wurtzite's homeopathic profile would focus on its ability to ground, balance, and energize, making it suitable for addressing conditions related to physical vitality and emotional stability.

Conclusion

Wurtzite is a powerful and versatile gemstone, cherished for its grounding, balancing, and energizing properties. Whether used for spiritual growth, physical healing, or enhancing overall well-being, Wurtzite serves as a potent aid in achieving a balanced and harmonious state. As with all alternative practices, these should be considered as complementary to conventional medical treatments.

Chapter Summary: Materia Medica

This chapter offers an extensive exploration into the spiritual, emotional, and physical healing properties of approximately 300 unique gemstones. This chapter is designed to provide a holistic understanding of how these gemstones can be utilized within homeopathic and alternative healing practices to promote overall well-being.

At the heart of gemstone homeopathy is the belief in the interconnectedness of the mind, body, and spirit. Each gemstone possesses unique vibrational frequencies that resonate with different aspects of human health. By leveraging these frequencies, practitioners aim to restore balance and harmony, addressing not only physical ailments but also emotional and spiritual imbalances. This approach recognizes that true healing encompasses all dimensions of the self, leading to a more profound and lasting well-being.

Many of the gemstones covered in this chapter are renowned for their ability to enhance spiritual growth and psychic abilities. Stones like Amethyst, Selenite, and Lapis Lazuli are highlighted for their capacity to open the third eye and crown chakras, facilitating deeper meditation, intuition, and spiritual awareness. These gemstones serve as powerful tools for those seeking to deepen their spiritual practice and connect with higher realms of consciousness. The chapter also explores how gemstones like Moldavite and Celestite can assist in astral travel and communication with spirit guides.

Emotional well-being is a significant focus in the Materia Medica. Gemstones such as Rose Quartz, Rhodochrosite, and Lepidolite are celebrated for their soothing and nurturing energies. They help release emotional blockages, heal past traumas, and foster a sense of love, compassion, and inner peace. The chapter provides detailed insights into how these stones can be used to support emotional healing and stability. Additionally, it discusses the role of gemstones like

Moonstone and Amazonite in balancing emotional states and promoting a calm, harmonious disposition.

Protection is a recurring theme throughout the chapter. Gemstones like Black Tourmaline, Hematite, and Smoky Quartz are known for their strong protective properties. They act as energetic shields, safeguarding the user from negative influences, psychic attacks, and electromagnetic pollution. The chapter elaborates on how these stones can be used to create a safe and secure environment for spiritual practices. Furthermore, it examines the protective roles of Obsidian and Shungite, which are particularly effective in grounding and detoxifying energies.

The physical healing attributes of gemstones are thoroughly explored. Stones such as Bloodstone, Carnelian, and Malachite are recognized for their ability to enhance vitality, support the immune system, and promote physical regeneration. The chapter offers comprehensive information on how these gemstones can aid in the recovery from illnesses, alleviate pain, and support overall physical health. It also covers how gemstones like Amber and Chrysocolla can aid in detoxification processes and improve respiratory health, providing a holistic approach to physical wellness.

Detoxification is another critical aspect covered in the Materia Medica. Gemstones like Fluorite, Apatite, and Chrysoprase are noted for their cleansing properties. They assist in purifying the body, mind, and spirit from toxins and negative energies. The chapter provides guidance on using these stones to support detoxification processes and maintain energetic purity. Additionally, it discusses the use of gemstones like Clear Quartz and Citrine in amplifying and focusing cleansing energies, making them indispensable tools in purification rituals.

The chapter emphasizes the importance of chakra balancing in holistic healing. Each gemstone is associated with specific chakras, helping to align and balance the body's energy centers. For example,

Citrine is linked to the solar plexus chakra, promoting confidence and personal power, while Aquamarine resonates with the throat chakra, enhancing communication and self-expression. The Materia Medica offers detailed instructions on using gemstones for chakra healing and alignment, including practical layouts and meditations for optimal energy flow.

Many gemstones are known for their ability to amplify energy, enhancing the effects of other healing practices. Clear Quartz, for instance, is often referred to as the "master healer" for its capacity to amplify the energy of other stones and intentions. The chapter delves into how these amplifying stones can be incorporated into healing rituals to boost their effectiveness. It also explores the synergistic effects of combining gemstones, such as using Amethyst and Rose Quartz together to enhance spiritual and emotional healing.

Each gemstone in the chapter is presented with a detailed homeopathic profile, outlining its psychological, physical, and behavioral indications. This includes descriptions of the symptoms and conditions that the gemstone can address, providing a practical guide for practitioners to select the appropriate stone for their needs. The profiles also highlight the unique energetic signatures of each gemstone, offering a deeper understanding of their healing potential. Special attention is given to rare and powerful gemstones like Phenacite and Larimar, which possess exceptional healing properties.

The chapter concludes with practical advice on incorporating gemstone remedies into daily life. This includes methods for wearing gemstones as jewelry, using them in meditation, placing them in living spaces, and creating gemstone elixirs. The guidance provided ensures that readers can effectively harness the healing properties of gemstones to enhance their well-being. Additionally, the chapter covers advanced techniques such as using gemstone grids for energy work and integrating gemstones into holistic therapies like Reiki and acupuncture.

In summary, the chapter on Materia Medica of gemstone homeopathic remedies is a comprehensive resource that encapsulates the rich diversity and profound healing potential of gemstones. It offers valuable insights into the spiritual, emotional, and physical benefits of gemstones, empowering readers to integrate these powerful tools into their holistic healing practices. This chapter serves as an essential guide for anyone interested in exploring the transformative power of gemstones and their applications in achieving overall well-being.

Also by Dr Víctor Denis Purcell

2
Materia Medica of Homeopathic Gemstones

Standalone
Zen and the Way of the Artist
Zen and the Art of Medicine
Zen and the Way of the Artist
The Yoga Book
Zen and the Art of Living and Dying
Zen and the Art of Photography
The Homeopathic Book
das homöopathische buch
El Libro De Homeopatía
Le Livre Homéopathique
The Traveler's Handbook
❖❖❖❖❖❖❖❖❖❖
"Architectural and Interior Design Mastery: A Global Perspective"
Medicinal Mushrooms
The New Testament
"Das Neue Testament, 2024"
Новый Завет
Mini Materia Medica

The Receptive Warrior
The God Center
The American Constitution
A Deep Dive Into Death
The Voyager's Odyssey
Mini Materia Medica
Mini Materia Medica
Spiritual Medicine: Materia Medica of Homeopathic Gemstones and Crystals
Spirituelle Medizin: Materia Medica der homöopathischen Edelsteine und Kristalle
Materia Medica of Homeopathic Gemstones
Médecine spirituelle Materia Medica des gemmes et cristaux homéopathiques
Materia Medica of Homeopathic Gemstones
Volume Two: Materia Medica of Homeopathic Gemstones
Volume Three: Materia Materia of Homeopathic Gemstones
Materia Medica of Homeopathic Gemstones: Volume Four

Also by Victor Denis Purcell

The Voyager's Odyssey
The Big Book of Tarot
Volume Two: Materia Medica of Homeopathic Gemstones
Materia Medica of Homeopathic Gemstones: Volume Four

About the Author

Victor Denis Purcell is a certified homeopathic practitioner with a master's degree in educational psychology. With a deep-rooted passion for homeopathic medicine, he has been actively involved in this field since 1982. Over the decades, he has authored numerous books covering a wide range of topics, demonstrating a profound understanding and expertise in homeopathic practices and holistic healing. Through a combination of professional experience and scholarly dedication, Victor Denis Purcell continues to contribute significantly to the advancement and awareness of homeopathic medicine.